Meet Your Planets offers an upbeat and fun approach to astrology. It introduces you to a totally new way of chart interpretation. Whether you're eighteen or eighty, you're sure to enjoy this humorous and insightful look at the zodiac!

Author Roy Alexander takes the wordiness out of the science of astrology and replaces the conventional discourses on planets, signs, houses, and aspects with colorful images you'll never forget. Alexander brings this lofty celestial information down to earth for the beginner and experienced astrologer alike.

In this amusing book, the planets are presented as an unforgettable lot of characters with very distinctive personalities and idiosyncrasies. Alexander turns the twelve traditional signs of the zodiac into 9-to-5 jobs so you can understand yourself and others by looking at the planets' actions and attitudes on the job. If a planet doesn't like its job, it will complain, procrastinate, throw a temper tantrum, pout—typical human behavior.

Now you can relate to the planets as people you know, work, and play with. These memorable characters will help you understand how to effectively use your strengths and how to overcome your weaknesses with this new and insightful astro-therapy for the 90s!

About the Author

Roy Alexander, an astrologer since 1970, has a degree in physics and is trained as a psychotherapist, mainly in the system of psychosynthesis, where much use is made of visual imagery. He was convinced early that astrology worked, but believed it didn't really help people to change. For twenty-five years, he has been concerned with making astrology more effective, and he believes that *Meet Your Planets* is the first really viable method. Roy has published two previous books and a number of articles in astrological magazines, and has spoken at various astrological events. He lives in London, where he had an astrological practice for ten years.

To Write to the Author

If you wish to contact the author or would like more information about this book, please write to him in care of Llewellyn Worldwide, and we will forward your request. Both the author and publisher appreciate hearing from you and learning of your enjoyment of this book and how it has helped you. Llewellyn Worldwide cannot guarantee that every letter written to the author can be answered, but all will be forwarded. Please write to:

Llewellyn Worldwide
P. O. Box 64383, Dept. K017–5
St. Paul, MN 55164-0383, U.S.A.

Please enclose a self-addressed, stamped envelope for reply, or $1.00 to cover costs.
If outside the U.S.A., enclose international postal reply coupon.

ROY ALEXANDER

MEET YOUR PLANETS

FUN WITH ASTROLOGY

Illustrations by Tom Grewe

1997
Llewellyn Publications
St. Paul, Minnesota 55164-0383, U.S.A.

FIRST EDITION
First Printing, 1997

Cover art and design: Tom Grewe
Illustrations: Tom Grewe
Book editing, design, and layout: Deb Gruebele
Project coordination: Connie Hill

Library of Congress Cataloging-in-Publication Data
    Alexander, Roy, 1931–
        Meet your planets : fun with astrology / Roy Alexander — 1st. ed.
            p.   cm.
        ISBN 1–56718–017–5
        1. Astrology.   2.   I. Title.
BL000.000   1997
000.00000—dc21   97–00000
                                                                      CIP

Printed in the United States of America.

Llewellyn Publications
A Division of Llewellyn Worldwide, Ltd.
St. Paul, Minnesota, 55164-0383, U.S.A.

Table of Contents

Acknowledgments   vi

How to Use This Book   vii

Bringing Your Chart to Life   1

Planets as People   11

Signs and Houses as Jobs   25

Sun in the Signs and Houses   41

Moon in the Signs and Houses   55

Mercury in the Signs and Houses   69

Venus in the Signs and Houses   83

Mars in the Signs and Houses   97

Jupiter in the Signs and Houses 111

Saturn in the Signs and Houses 125

Uranus in the Signs and Houses 139

Neptune in the Signs and Houses 155

Pluto in the Signs and Houses 169

Aspects 183

How We Cope with Our Planets 203

Appendix A: Working with the Characters 213

Appendix B: The Astrological Universe 217

Acknowledgments

This material first appeared in a very abbreviated form in the British magazine *PREDICTION*.

The examples of chart positions scattered throughout the text have been taken from many sources, not now readily identifiable. Some of them were taken, with thanks, from *The American Book of Charts* by Lois M. Rodden, published by Astro Computing Services, 1980.

How to Use This Book

This book contains detailed interpretations of planets in signs and houses, and by aspect. These interpretations are not, in themselves, very important. They can be useful in delineating a chart, but they are mainly there to make you think and to encourage you to look at the deeper levels of meaning shown by the images from which the interpretations are derived.

You may already have looked up the interpretations of some of your chart positions and perhaps found them not very flattering. Don't take them too literally. At best, these kinds of delineations are only a ballpark shot. Try to get to the spirit behind the words and meditate on the image that is given rather than being concerned about whether you "are" the sort of person indicated.

It is a great weakness of astrology that it tends to define people—for example, you have Moon in Cancer, *therefore* you *are* clinging, oversensitive, or shy. It may or may not be true that you are manifesting these qualities in the world. What is true is that, at a slightly deeper level, you have a quality of energy that can be pictured as a patient, caring housekeeper looking after a baby. By focusing your attention on *that* rather than the outer "symptoms," you can begin to open up feeling and behavior patterns that you may have become stuck in. Not that there will be any instant shift; it will be more like lighting a long fuse, as a client of mine once put it.

This is the main point of the system of astrology presented here, not to provide another set of delineations, but to offer a way of going beyond them. Whether you are reading your own chart or working with a client, use the conventional delineations to get a fix on a problem, and then forget them. Go to the images. Look at the character who is causing the problem as he or she tries to do two jobs and to relate to some of the other planetary characters.

In this way, you don't have to be fazed by even the most negative "reading." One can talk about transcending one's planets, but that is not easy to do. In practice, planets that are in difficult signs, houses, or aspects are frequently a source of more or less unmitigated stress and psychic pain. We all have such unfortunately placed planets. Instead of battling with them and trying to repress the pain, the system presented in this book offers a way of understanding and making friends with the planetary energies. This is much more likely to result in genuine transcendence of their effects at the level of the personality.

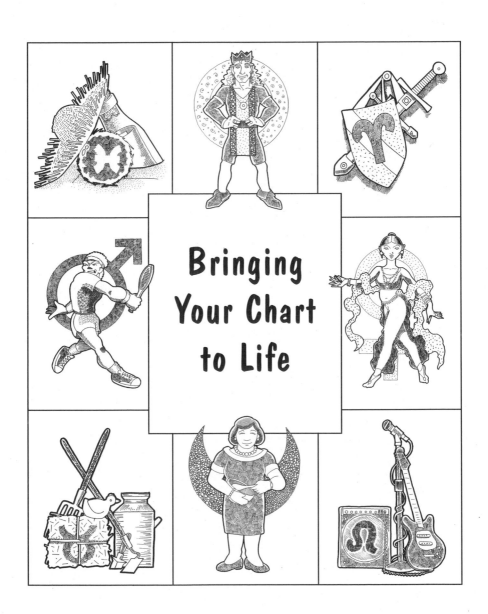

Bringing Your Chart to Life

Astrology as a Tool

Astrology is a great diagnostic tool. We don't understand how it works, but a good astrologer can interpret your birth chart in such a way that it is an almost complete X-ray picture of your personality, and even of your unconscious patterns. A detailed astrological analysis can provide you with a lifetime's guidance and show you many things about yourself that you may be surprised to discover.

However, if all this remains at the level of intellectual information, it will not make much difference. The analysis, by itself, will have no power to change your life and that, after all, is what most of us are looking for. If you have a couple of planets in Virgo, let us say, the chart reading will most likely point out that you are much inclined to worry. Merely knowing this doesn't make you less of a worrier, any more than knowing the technical name for a stomachache makes the pain go away.

Often, after an initial enthusiastic encounter with astrology, people realize that they are still the same and become disillusioned. We live in a world in which intellectual knowledge is highly prized while imagination, feeling, and intuition are little regarded. We automatically assume that the answer to any problem is to be found in obtaining more information about it. The reaction of some astrologers to the fact that an astrological analysis doesn't help people to really change their lives has been to search for better techniques and more information. There are more techniques available now than any single person can use.

Calculations that were once complicated and tedious can now be performed by computers. You can have your chart set up in half a dozen different systems with analyses by midpoints, phase relationships, hypothetical planets, harmonics, and several other techniques. All of these things can be very valuable for further and more precise diagnosis, but the result is that you have more and more information about yourself that still doesn't change the way you are. Indeed, a person may often not be able to recognize and relate to much of the material in the analysis.

Other astrologers have tried to remedy the situation by turning to techniques of psychotherapy. The chart is used to diagnose a particular problem, and once the client is aware of the issue, the counselor uses therapeutic techniques to work on it and attempt to resolve it. This is the approach I used myself. I would conduct a detailed analysis of the chart using midpoints and phase relationships before seeing the client. Then, after identifying a problem the client needed to work on, I would put the chart aside and use a form of existential counseling. This worked, but it was very time-consuming and demanded a certain kind of commitment from the client that not everyone was prepared to make. I eventually became dissatisfied with the method because it was not really making use of astrology. The counseling technique could be used with any other system of diagnosis.

The Mythological Approach

Another group of astrologers has sought to make chart analysis more effective by relating astrology to mythology. The thinking is, more or less, that if you have a problem with a particular sign or planet, you can more imaginatively relate to that sign or planet if you know the myths associated with it. Again, this approach works. It enables the client to understand his or her chart at the level of feeling and imagination, rather than just head knowledge.

The mythological approach can be combined with the psychotherapeutic one, but it is open to much the same objections, the first being that the astrological chart has to be discarded in favor of something else. Again, too, it requires a commitment on the part of the client to research and meditate on the relevant myth. Not everyone is turned on by mythology, so again, the application of the method is somewhat limited.

What the therapeutic and the mythological approaches have in common is that they seek to translate a chart reading from a verbal experience into a feeling or imaginative one. This is indeed the key to actual change. Let's say you have a powerful emphasis on Aries in your chart. The plain chart interpretation will say something like, "You are active, restless, and pushy, with a pioneering spirit and the need to feel that you are always the first in anything."

So far, so good. Most people will read that, or whatever applies to them, and say, "Yes, that's true." and then go on being pushy or whatever without resolving the problem the analysis identified.

The therapeutic approach would have the person get specific about experiences of being dominant and thrusting, and see what feelings and body sensations go with the experiences. In this way, the interpretation goes beyond a verbal description that is merely head knowledge and begins to come alive in a meaningful way.

The mythological approach might do the same thing, and also require that the person meditate on the myth of Jason and the golden fleece, which can be seen as an Aries myth. In this way, the person will get closer to the archetype of Aries. The experience of the interpretation will go beyond the superficial level of words, which have little power to change anything, and into the deeper levels of the psyche, where change is possible.

Another point here is that astrology, like particle physics, has its own principle of indeterminacy. In physics, it is impossible to know precisely both the position and momentum of an electron, to take one example. The more accurately you measure the position, the vaguer the momentum becomes, and the other way around. Likewise, in astrology, the more specific you get about some factor, the less likely it is to be true of any given individual.

We've already had the example of a person with a strong Aries, and we suggested words like "pushy, restless, active, and dominating" as suitable descriptions for the person. However, they won't apply to everyone with planets in Aries. In perhaps eight or nine out of ten cases they will, but you can always find some people with strong Aries who, on the face of it at least, are reserved and diffident. If you get even more specific and say that Aries will always drive fast and wear something red, both of which are certainly expressions of Aries, the chances of this description being accurate for any particular Aries person are quite low.

Often, of course, the chart itself will indicate how expressive a given factor might be. Sun in Aries in the Twelfth House conjunct Saturn will be a lot more muted than Sun in Aries in the First House conjunct Mars. Even so, you can still find examples of a technically strong Aries planet that doesn't come out in the way you would expect.

We are talking here about levels of manifestation. The Sun, or another planet, in Aries will be evident at some level in the person's life, but the quality may be there only as a sort of wordless background "tone" and not be manifest in the behavior or personality at all. In this case, the person will not be able to recognize the sort of definition we have used.

This is where the use of mythology can be helpful. By meditating on the appropriate myth, the person may be able to get in touch with his or her Aries qualities and allow them to manifest more fully in the world.

After years of experience, and trying a number of counseling techniques, it seemed to me that what was needed was a way of translating the verbal delineations of astrology directly into visual images. The result is the system presented in this book.

The idea was put into my mind by a passage in one of Dane Rudhyar's books. I can't find it now and don't think it referred to planets in signs and houses. Translated into those terms, however, it came down to this— a planet is like the President, the sign is the Office of the Presidency, and the house is the President's office, or the White House, if you like.

From there it was a short step to see that a planet could be a person, the sign a job that he or she has to do, and the house a situation in which the person finds himself or herself. This idea is capable of some very subtle nuances in chart interpretation, but for the purposes of this book I have chosen to treat signs and houses as being the same thing.

The Characters and The Jobs

We begin by turning the planets into characters. They are:
- The Sun—a King
- The Moon—a Housekeeper/Secretary
- Mercury—a Computer Whiz Kid
- Venus—a Temple Dancer
- Mars—a Tennis Champion
- Jupiter—your Favorite Uncle
- Saturn—an Old Math Teacher
- Uranus—a Crazy Inventor
- Neptune—a Romantic Poet
- Pluto—a Magician

The first seven are seen as real people; the last three as cartoon figures, for reasons that will be explained later.

Now that we have our planetary characters, we have to find them jobs to do to represent the combined houses and signs. These can be:
- Aries—a Knight Errant
- Taurus—a Farmer
- Gemini—a News Reporter

Cancer—a Baby Sitter
Leo—a Pop Star
Virgo—a Doctor
Libra—a Maitre d'
Scorpio—a Private Eye
Sagittarius—an Explorer
Capricorn—a Business Executive
Aquarius—a Social Worker
Pisces—a Castaway on a Desert Island

Obviously, these choices are fairly arbitrary and, in practice, the jobs sometimes have to be changed slightly to bring out the qualities of a particular planet more effectively. The point is that now we have vivid images in place of the verbal descriptions, and these images cut much more deeply. One of the most striking examples is Mars in Libra. Here we have the hard-hitting Tennis Champion, something like John McEnroe, having to earn a living as an obsequious, deferential maitre d' of a classy restaurant. The frustrations he will experience are obvious and the image makes the energy of Mars in Libra or Seventh House much easier to understand than the conventional verbal delineations.

Most of the rest of the book consists of descriptions of the characters doing their various jobs together with the more conventional delineations of the effect on the person. In this way, the effect of the planet, in sign or house, on the personality is seen as a kind of fallout of the planetary character trying to do his or her job, actually two jobs, except with early Aries rising and equal houses. The planets also have to get along with each other, as shown by the aspects, which will be dealt with more briefly.

This scheme has the advantages of a mythological approach to the chart without having to go outside the chart itself. There is nothing in this book that is not traditional astrology; it offers merely a different language and a different perspective.

Using This Book to Your Advantage

The next two chapters introduce the planets as characters and the signs/houses as jobs. The rest of the book deals with how well the planetary characters do their various jobs and how well they get along with each other. What we have is seven highly individualistic people, the traditional planets, and three even more individualistic maniacs, the outer planets, all absorbed in their own affairs, sometimes helping each other and sometimes getting in each other's way. All this uproar among the planets is what we experience as the way we live our lives.

For each planet, there will first of all be a description of the character doing the job, and the problems or pleasures that he or she encounters. Second will be a description of what we are likely to experience down here in the world as a result of the character's efforts. These second descriptions will be much the same kind of delineations of planets in houses and signs that you will get in other astrology books. They must be general because nothing will work in exactly the same way in two different people. We all have a unique combination of planetary energies. Even identical twins will have some small differences in their birth charts.

The most important thing, then, is to get the feeling of the character doing the job. I would suggest the best way to use this book is to read it through, paying most attention to the descriptions of the characters doing their jobs. See if you can empathize with him or her and imagine what it would be like to be that character. Try to get the feel of what life is like for each of them, what it's like for a Temple Dancer to be a business executive or a King to be a pop star. As you do this, your understanding of the planet in sign or house will move away from the superficial, verbal level and toward the archetypal level. You will begin to understand the astrological factors more deeply and, in the case of your own chart, yourself more deeply.

When you have the feel of the character doing his or her job, you will be able to see why each placement means what it does. Then read the delineation and see how it fits you or someone you know with that combination of planet/sign/house. Don't take the interpretations too literally, but rather try to get to the spirit behind them. The conventional, verbal interpretations given after each description of a planet at work should be seen to follow naturally from the efforts of the planet to do the job.

If you learn to think in terms of the images, it will improve your skill as an astrologer because it will enable you to work from the "feel" of a planet in a sign or house and not just the verbal description of it. More than that, as you get a feeling sense of the planet, the outer manifestation will change to some extent. If you have Venus in Aquarius, for example, and find that a tendency to be too detached in relationships is causing you problems, get into the feel of what it is like for the Temple Dancer to be a social worker.

You don't have to do anything about it, just open yourself to the aware-ness of what is going on at that level, slightly below normal consciousness. Although the planetary characters are fictitious, the energies within us are real enough. To say that our planets appreciate a bit of sympathy and understanding, just like anybody else, is accurate, if metaphorical. If you have Mars in Libra and you have trouble with suppressed anger, spare a thought now and then for the poor guy having to earn his crust as the maitre d'. Once Mars realizes that you are aware of what he has to put up with, your relationship with him will change. Over a period of time, you will find that suppressed anger and other Mars in Libra problems will at least loosen up, if not entirely go away.

Obviously, a whole system of astrotherapy can be developed from this idea. Practicing astrocounselors may want to experiment with it as a way of assisting their clients; but the system can be of use to everybody, whether you are an experienced astrologer, a student, or somebody who has just had their chart read for the first time.

In choosing the planetary characters, I have tried to reflect the way the planets are used and thought of in current astrological practice. Some people will find the resulting proportion of eight men to two women unsatisfactory. There is no real reason the characters have to be the sex I have given them. Any of the male characters could equally well be a woman. The female characters could be men, but, though I can think of a male for the Moon (valet, butler, or something like that), I can't think of a suitable male character for Venus. It was hard enough to think of a suitable female!

If you find that some other character or some other job fits your under-standing better and works better for you, then use that rather than the one given. The system is meant to be a key to accessing *your* imagination. Astrology is not an objective science. It is an art and a language, and we each need to use it in our own individual way.

Planets

as

People

Sun ☉

King

The energy of the Sun is the very center of life within us. It's that force that inspires us to go on living, like the fire in a boiler or electricity stored in a battery. It is a limitless creative power, and the physical sun, which pours out more energy in a single second than our minds can grasp, is an apt symbol of such power. When we are in the Sun mode, we feel strong, capable, even heroic.

The image for the Sun is a King. He is about thirty-five, strong, handsome, and highly charismatic, more like a storybook king than a real one. He is King Arthur, Shakespeare's Henry V—a hero figure. He is king because everyone naturally admires him and looks up to him, not by any kind of force.

Yet we should still think of him as a human being. He has his weaknesses; he still needs to learn and grow. There is something of the performer about him and he has to appear strong, certain, and in control all the time, even when he doesn't feel any of these things. It is part of his job to inspire confidence and optimism in his people, to assure them that all is well and that the realm is secure and prosperous, so he can function properly only when he is recognized and acknowledged. He has to be visible—he can't work behind the scenes—and he needs his people as much as they need him. Applause keeps him going.

☽ Moon

Housekeeper/ Secretary

The Moon is that power that takes care of us. She lets us know when we should eat and sleep and otherwise look after ourselves. The Sun inspires us to go on living and the Moon sees to the practical business of it. It is Moon energy that motivates us to carry out all the habitual, more or less unconscious, actions and patterns that get us through the day. Her province is all the instincts, including sexuality. When the Moon is moving us, we like to stay with routine, familiar things, though some people's idea of routine might be mountain climbing or parachute jumping!

There are a lot of images we might use for the Moon. She has so many faces she is difficult to pin down, like the changing Moon in the sky. A useful image is a sort of Housekeeper/Secretary to the King. She also works a bit of magic on the side when it is needed.

The Housekeeper/Secretary is also about thirty-five. She is thorough, patient, and caring. She deals with all the King's appointments and correspondence. She also oversees all the domestic arrangements for the palace, making sure the meals are cooked, the children taken care of, and the place kept in good repair. Most of what she does can be seen by anyone, but once in a while she puts on a white robe, goes to a lonely tower, and performs secret rituals that help keep up her strength, courage, and endurance.

Mercury ☿

Computer Whiz Kid

The energy of Mercury is what makes us think, what makes us interested and curious. Mercury pushes us to find out what's going on, to learn all kinds of skills. He is the pressure for knowledge and communication, which includes traveling and being sociable, though Mercury contacts are mostly mental ones. When we are in the Mercury mode, we are inquisitive, talkative, sometimes anxious and nervous.

The image for Mercury is the Computer Whiz Kid. He is about sixteen years old with a genius-level IQ and a photographic memory. He has built his own computer with a lot of improved functions. When he is not reading technical books and magazines, or working with his computer, he is discussing technical matters with his fellow whiz kids.

Though the Computer Whiz Kid is brilliant intellectually and practically, he is naive and hopeless when it comes to feelings. They embarrass him and don't have much reality for him. He loves solving problems and outsmarting people. The Whiz Kid has all the adolescent's prickly pride and defensiveness. It is hard for him to admit that he might be wrong about anything. It is not that he has no feelings, but that his feelings have been totally repressed. Without his logic, reason, and sense of being practical, he thinks he would not exist, so he clings to them at any cost.

♀ Venus

Temple Dancer

The energy of Venus moves us to enjoy pleasure of all kinds, but especially emotional and physical pleasure. To understand Venus properly, we need to realize that such pleasure is essential to life. We tend to think of pleasure as something that should come second to work and duty. Yet, if we get no Venus pleasure, we become ineffective. The true Venus pleasure is a deep sense of physical, emotional, and mental well-being. Most people probably experience this only after making love, which is why Venus is the love goddess. When we are in the Venus mode, we feel sociable, sexy, and inclined to amusement and entertainment.

Finding a character to represent Venus is not easy because of the attitude toward love and pleasure we have just looked at. The image I have chosen for Venus is far removed from Western society with its Puritan Work Ethic. She is a Temple Dancer from ancient India.

We can imagine her as a very beautiful young Indian girl. Everything she wears, every movement and gesture, is designed to express sexuality. She is highly skilled in lovemaking, dancing, and other arts of pleasure. An encounter with her is enchanting, taking us out of this world. The Temple Dancer is willing to entertain and make love with any man who comes to the temple, provided it is done as a way of paying homage to the forces of nature. To understand her, we have to drop all the unfortunate ideas about exploitation that cluster about the image of unfettered sexuality.

Mars ♂

Tennis Champion

The energy of Mars is aggression and assertion. Mars is what makes us compete and "go for it," but not necessarily in a spectacular way. Any sort of definite action is Mars, even something that looks as quiet as putting words on paper. We usually experience Mars as feeling courageous and determined, wanting to get things done and to win, or feeling angry and ready to fight.

Unlike Venus, Mars is highly regarded in our society and it is not difficult to think of a number of images for him. I've chosen a Tennis Champion (TC); smashing home a thunderbolt ace service is about as Mars as you can get.

The Tennis Champion never lets up, never gets bored or tired, and never lets anybody get the better of him if he can possibly help it. To him, winning is everything and losing is nothing. He can drive himself on and on, knowing that stamina and endurance are as vital as skill in winning matches.

Relationships are not very important to him. His motto is "He travels the fastest who travels alone." He is interested in other people only so far as they can advance his career or teach him new skills. The Tennis Champion is an explosive, touchy character, always game for a fight or a challenge, as ready to argue with the umpire as play tennis.

♃ Jupiter

Favorite Uncle

The energy of Jupiter makes us expand our horizons, go for something bigger and better than what we have. He also makes us want to be socially successful, to have a definite place in the community, and be recognized and looked up to. With Jupiter at work in us, we feel benevolent, lucky, and tolerant. The expansion can take many forms, from putting a bet on a horse to enrolling in a course in philosophy!

The image for Jupiter is your Favorite Uncle. He is a man of about fifty, friendly and easy-going. I like to see him as bearded and smoking a pipe. Favorite Uncle is rich and knows a great deal about the world. He knows everybody and has the sort of confidence and charisma that get him the best seats at the theater, the best attention in the most expensive restaurants.

Favorite Uncle has wisdom as well as knowledge, unlike Computer Whiz Kid, with whom he shares great curiosity and interest in life. He understands everyone's point of view and is as much at home with feelings as with logic. He is always willing to offer guidance from his rich and varied experience, but does not force any of his views on you. It goes without saying that he enjoys the good things in life. He likes to throw big parties at his fabulous ranch home where the food and wine, the company and the entertainment, are always first class.

Saturn ♄

Old Math Teacher

Saturn makes us face our responsibilities, our limitations, and the consequences of our actions. Most of us don't enjoy doing this, so Saturn is an unpopular planet. When we are in the grip of Saturn, we usually feel restricted and blocked, frustrated because we can't have what we want right NOW! More positively, when Saturn is affecting us, we are able to be realistic and settle down to hard work. Even so, if we have been carried away by the benevolence of Jupiter, the experience of Saturn is unpleasant.

There are many possible images for Saturn. A grim and forbidding policeman would be one. More useful for our purposes is a dried-up, austere Old Math Teacher (OMT). The point of choosing mathematics is that it is a cut-and-dried subject with no room for personal opinion. Everything has to be proved; every equation has to be worked out.

The OMT lives according to these standards. He is precise, dry, inclined to be sarcastic, and concerned only with accuracy and proof. If your work is correct, you will get good grades from him, but don't expect praise or encouragement! He makes no concessions to personal charm, difficult circumstances, or poor health. Either your equations are worked out correctly or they are not; there is no middle way. As far as the Old Math Teacher is concerned, everything is already known and the rules laid down. He wouldn't recognize a new viewpoint no matter what the evidence for it.

The Traditional Versus Outer Planets

These descriptions of the seven traditional planets of astrology are more or less idealizations. The planets don't always behave like this. It helps in understanding them to keep in mind that they are just as complex as human beings.

The King feels timid and insecure now and then, and the Housekeeper will sometimes get drunk and go on a rampage, smashing dishes in the kitchen. The Computer Whiz Kid will date a girl occasionally, while the Temple Dancer likes to relax by solving crossword puzzles and chess problems. Even the Tennis Champion will go out of his way to be kind to stray kitties. Favorite Uncle has a cheap streak and will sometimes steal hotel towels. The Old Math Teacher's secret vice is to weep during sentimental movies.

Uranus, Neptune and Pluto are more like caricatures or cartoon figures. They are much more rigid and obsessed with their particular act and are more than a little overpowering from a human point of view. For one of these planets to behave out of character would be like Donald Duck acting reasonable! When they interact with the traditional planets, it is like a movie with mixed live action and cartoon figures. We will think of them as people, but remember they have this dimension of manic weirdness.

Uranus ⛢

Crazy Inventor

The main function of Uranus is to get us to see things differently. He is a great destroyer of blinders, dogma, and any situation that has become fossilized and no longer useful. He operates all the time on lateral thinking. If we want to hold on to what we have, fossilized or not, Uranus can seem dangerous and destructive. When we are in the Uranus mode, we are rebellious and full of new ideas, wanting to chuck everything and make a fresh start.

The image for Uranus is the Crazy Inventor. See him as a cartoon figure of a man in his mid-thirties, with wild eyes and a manic smile. He is untidy, with his hair all over the place. He wears odd socks and has a calculator sticking out of his pocket.

The Crazy Inventor is the complete opposite of Saturn. He obeys no rules, or rather, he regards all rules and conventions merely as more or less useful operating instructions that can always be discarded. He is highly eccentric. His motto is "Expect the unexpected." Absolutely nothing whatsoever is taken for granted. Given a chance, he will question even life and death or the power of gravity. The Crazy Inventor is not a comfortable person to have around, but he is certainly stimulating.

Ψ Neptune

Romantic Poet

The aim of Neptune is hard to define. At one level, you can say that he just wants to sit and let the world go by, accepting and enjoying everything as it comes along. To Neptune, everything is as important as everything else; to him, a microbe is no less significant than a galaxy. This is not a state of mind that human beings normally experience. So we know Neptune only dimly. We usually feel him as moods of being spacey and dreamy, with vague longings for something we know we want but can't quite pin down.

The image for Neptune, again a cartoon figure, is the Romantic Poet. He looks rather like John Keats. He is a little drunk. See him as a young man in his early twenties, wearing nineteenth-century clothes with a big, floppy collar on his shirt. He is sitting in a dimly lit room listening to a nightingale. His mind is full of images that the bird's song has conjured up, and he is not aware of his physical surroundings. He imagines the nightingale so vividly that he has almost become the bird.

The Romantic Poet is hardly aware of having a personality or personal identity. He is so powerfully affected by everything that happens to him that he mentally and emotionally takes the shape of it, as if he were modeling clay. He has no interest in permanent structures or patterns; he wants only to flow with the experience of the present moment.

The nature of Pluto is even more difficult to understand than that of Neptune. It's not that difficult to put into words, but the words themselves have such vast meanings. Pluto wants total and ultimate power and knowledge. He wants to understand the secret forces of the universe and how to work with them. When Pluto is affecting us, we want to control things, get to a deep understanding of life, or to be top-dog and boss a lot of people around. These are all rather unusual states, and many people may never experience them at all.

Pluto is the Magician, again a cartoon figure. He is about forty, very physically, mentally, and emotionally vigorous. He has passed through ordeals and initiations that the rest of us can hardly even imagine. He wears a violet robe decorated with the signs of the zodiac. He stands in a magic circle holding a sword. In a triangle outside the circle, a spirit has appeared. The Magician has conjured it, and it will do anything he demands.

The Magician has great power, but he needs to be motivated by the law of love or he will do himself more harm than good. If he does not obey the law of love, the power will be taken away from him.

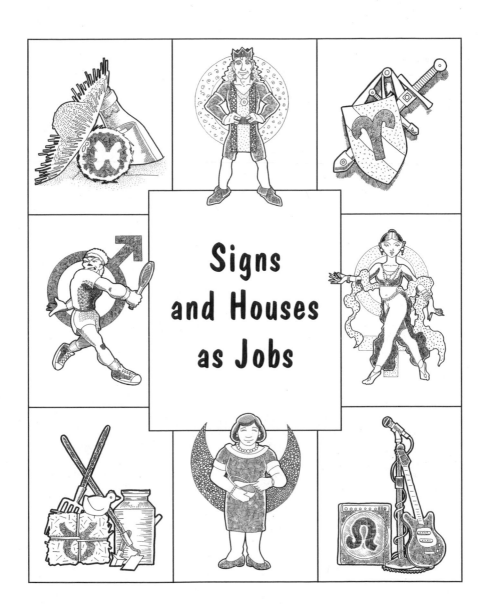

Signs
and Houses
as Jobs

The Significance of Planetary Placings

We are now going to look at the jobs the ten planetary characters have to do. These jobs represent the combined meanings of the twelve signs and houses. To treat the sign of the zodiac and the corresponding house as being the same is an approximation. A planet in Aries is not exactly the same as a planet in the First House.

Broadly, you can say that the signs are characteristics of the person and the houses the kinds of issues that he or she has to confront in life. House placings tend to be more compulsive; they show issues the person will be brought back to again and again. I would go so far as to say that, far from the Sun sign being the most significant placing, as popular astrology would have us believe, the dominant factor in a person's life is the house position of the Moon.

The distinction between signs and houses can be important in a consultation, but they are similar enough to be treated as one for our purposes. As a rule of thumb, you can add, say, fifty percent extra weight to a house placing as distinct from its corresponding sign.

First of all, we shall see what the sign/house means, and then devise an appropriate job for it. For most of the sign/house meanings, one job will do, but sometimes we will need a second one to bring out better the qualities of the way the planet does the job. This is especially true of Libra. I've used three jobs for Libra, though they all have to do with maintaining harmony or creating a balance.

The descriptions in this chapter will be brief. Later on, we will encounter ten different views of each job as we see how the planets cope with them.

The way of looking at the planets described in this book treats them as human beings. Just like real people, planets in jobs they don't like will try to get out of doing them. Sometimes, especially in the case of the Moon/Housekeeper, they will *overdo* them out of conscientiousness. Saturn is another planet who will be likely to be over-conscientious about doing jobs he doesn't like.

The effect on the person will be that they will either not seem to have any of the qualities of the sign/house or that they will have a surplus. For example, Mars hates being in Libra so much that the person with this placing may not seem to have any of the charm, sociability, or indecisiveness of Libra. On the other hand, the Moon doesn't like being in Libra either, but she will do the job conscientiously, and the person with this placing may seem very Libra indeed.

We are touching here on a problem with astrology that we can't go into very deeply in this book. It is that we all block off some parts of ourselves and overemphasize others. As we grow up, we develop a fairly stable image of who we are that enables us to fit in with the world about us. This image is described by the Ascendant of the chart, which we will look at later. Very roughly speaking, we will deny things about ourselves that do not easily fit with the Ascendant image and make great play with the ones that do.

Then, there is the factor already noted that the houses seem more compulsive than the signs. The house is the job the planet will attend to *first*. If the planet has a hard time coping with the house, it won't have as much energy for the sign as you might expect.

For example, you would expect someone with Moon in Cancer to be very warm and motherly, good at caring for people, always surrounded by children and pets. But if the Moon is in the Sixth or Eighth or Tenth Houses, all of which are very difficult for her, she won't have much energy left for the Cancer job. There won't be nearly as much of the typical Cancer quality in the person as you would think.

If it is the other way around, and the Moon is in the Second or Fourth Houses, which are jobs she does with no trouble, then, if she is in Scorpio or Capricorn, she will have more energy for the sign, and its characteristics will probably be very marked in the person. In general, the house should be given more weight than the sign in interpretation, though this can't be taken as a hard and fast rule. Experience is the best guide.

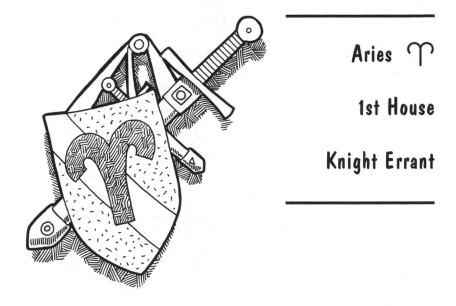

The main requirement of the Aries job is to develop personal courage and individual excellence. The qualities a planet must have to do the job are initiative and self-assertiveness. He or she must be willing to take on all challenges and be able to crank up enthusiasm for a fight in nothing flat. Act first and think (if at all) afterward is what is needed here. And, as well as bravery, the planet needs personal integrity of a very male, macho kind.

The job that fits Aries/First House is being a Knight Errant. The whole idea of living by a Code of Honor, going off alone on dangerous quests, fighting dragons, and rescuing damsels in distress is pure Aries. So is the idea of attacking all opposition with all-out, reckless courage rather than by clever tactics. Winning by means of a cleverly-thought-out campaign is not much better than cheating and treachery to your true Knight Errant. He or she would rather lose honorably to a better knight.

The King and the Tennis Champion are best suited to the Aries job.

♉ Taurus

2nd House

Farmer

This job is about stability. The requirements of the Taurus/Second House job are to put down roots, stay in the same place, and make something of it. Endurance, patience, and perseverance are the qualities at work in Taurus/Second House. A planet doing this job must be good at getting material results. Being practical and reliable is needed here, with a good sense of having both feet on the ground.

Farming is the job for most planets. This is an old-fashioned Farmer who works by long familiarity with the soil, the weather, and the seasons. He or she doesn't have modern technology and doesn't need it. In fact, such newfangled stuff would do more harm than good. The family has farmed the land for centuries and knows exactly what works and what doesn't to get the maximum yield from it, so the Farmer is not interested in new ideas. The old ones work well and he or she sees no sense in changing for the sake of it to something that might *not* work. Security is always uppermost in the Farmer's mind. He or she knows it takes hard work to make a living, and can't risk change.

The Housekeeper and the Temple Dancer are both good at this job because they are attuned to earthy rhythms. For the Temple Dancer, though, we'll think of her as Manager of a *health* farm. Favorite Uncle does the job quite well, too.

The main needs of this job are lively, monkey-like curiosity and activity, and a love of news and gossip. Learning is the keynote of Gemini, in the sense of gathering facts, but not reflecting much on what they might mean. Another Gemini creature is the magpie. To this bird, all bright objects are of equal value, and a planet doing the Gemini job must be able to see all snippets of news and information as equally interesting.

The natural job for Gemini is the News Reporter. He or she has to keep alert and alive, be prepared to follow up any leads, and is never off duty, as anything could turn into an interesting story. The News Reporter can't afford to let feelings get in the way of the job. The story must be told, and the pieces will fall where they may. It's not the *News Reporter's* responsibility if somebody gets damaged by such fearless exposure of the facts.

The Talk Show Host is also a good Gemini job. This job requires the same qualities as the News Reporter, but allows the planet to be, or seem, a little more sociable and genial.

Computer Whiz Kid is the one who does this job best. It's too unfeeling or superficial for most of the others.

♋ Cancer

4th House

Baby Sitter

The Cancer job is about creating a safe, nurturing environment where living things can grow. It is like the Taurus job, but Cancer is much more sensitive and delicate. Both are concerned with security, but Taurus takes it more for granted. Taurus is mainly concerned with things for his or her own use. Cancer is also very possessive, but more sympathetically and emotionally concerned with other creatures' well-being.

The ideal job for Cancer would be a mother, but this would hardly work for the male characters. However, we can choose the nearest substitute and make the Cancer job a Baby Sitter. Obviously, the Baby Sitter has to be concerned mainly with the baby. To do the job well, the planetary character has to be in tune with instincts, intuitions, and feelings. It's no good telling the baby that she shouldn't be hungry for another two hours according to the schedule, or that it isn't *logical* to cry because she has just thrown her rattle out of reach.

The Baby Sitter has to be constantly alert, not only to the baby's needs, but to anything else that can go wrong. Is the baby about to poke a knife into the electric socket or pull a kettle of boiling water over herself? Why has she turned blue? It's a stressful job. Only the Housekeeper does it really well, though Favorite Uncle is a good second.

Leo is about total self-expression. To do the Leo job, a planet has to enjoy being the center of attention, but in such a way that he or she gives back a lot of love and energy. If Cancer was the job for the mother, then in one sense, Leo is the father; in this case, a jovial, big-hearted father who knows how to keep the kids happy because he is still half a kid himself.

The father image won't work for the female characters, so a star entertainer who is loved for his or her warmth and personality is a good image for Leo. The bigger the audience, the better Leo likes it, so we will say that the Leo job is being a Pop Star. A planet in this job has to *act* big, but also mean it at the same time. Unless the character enjoys what he or she is doing and loves the audience quite genuinely, the performance won't come off. It is a tricky balance because if the planet is doing the Leo job well, the reward is so much adulation that it is almost bound to go to the Pop Star's head. So, though Leo is really about love, it can easily get turned into a power trip. If the Pop Star starts to believe the audience needs him or her more than he or she needs them, there is trouble.

Being the Pop Star is very much like being the King, who is the only one who does the job really well.

♍ Virgo

6th House

Doctor

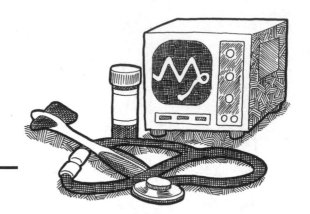

One way of looking at this job is to say that Virgo has to clean up after Leo. Leo can't be bothered with details, whereas Virgo thinks about nothing else. For Virgo, everything goes by facts and logic. To rely on warmth and personality, as Leo does, appalls Virgo. For this sign, things have to be done by the book, with every last detail accounted for.

A good job for Virgo is a Doctor, of the formal, arid, old-fashioned kind, one who never jokes with patients or displays anything close to a warm bedside manner. In fact, this Doctor doesn't really regard patients as human beings, but as collections of symptoms that he or she was trained to deal with. This Doctor enjoys doing the paperwork—seeing patients at all is a reluctant concession to reality. Preferred practice would be to run a list of symptoms through the computer to produce a prescription, but it won't work because the patients can't be believed anyway, so an examination is necessary, distasteful as that is. If only everyone else were as careful and logical, the Doctor thinks, there would be a lot less trouble.

Computer Whiz Kid is the character who does this job best.

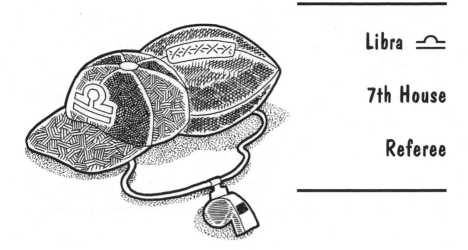

Libra ♎

7th House

Referee

This job is about keeping everybody happy, seeing that justice is done and is *seen* to be done. A planet doing this job has to put the interests of other people first and back pedal on his or her own self-assertiveness. In some ways, Libra needs to combine the almost incompatible qualities of Leo and Virgo, paying attention to the facts, yet relying on warmth of personality.

Any job that involves keeping a balance is Libra. A Referee of some kind is a good image. So is a Diplomat, a Party Hostess, or a Maitre d'. All these jobs are about being fair and trying to please everybody—an impossible task. A bit less obviously, the jobs are also about creating patterns, making sure that various pieces of experience match up, and especially, responding to pressures as they happen. This tends to mean that Libra often seems indecisive, changeable, or downright two-faced. What, for example, is the Maitre d' to do when, after he or she has accepted a tip to give someone the best table, another customer offers an even bigger tip?

The character who does this job best is the Temple Dancer because she is trained to please herself in pleasing others. The Old Math Teacher is good at it too because he thinks pleasing himself is self indulgent anyway, and he looks on the job as making the equations come out.

♏ Scorpio

8th House

Private Eye

The Scorpio job is about dealing with the darker side of life. Scorpio likes, or rather feels compelled, to poke about in the distasteful secrets the rest of us prefer not to know about. This is very isolating, and a planet doing the Scorpio job needs plenty of stamina and determination to go his or her own way.

A good job for Scorpio is the Private Eye. He or she can be a fictional detective like Philip Marlowe or Mike Hammer, but has to be tough and incorruptible, and can't afford to scare easily or be seduced by power, money, or sex. The job demands that he or she should resist all temptations in favor of the ideal of discovering the truth. In some ways, the job is like the Knight Errant gone a little sleazy!

Scorpio tends to be strong and silent, with a vigilante's sense of justice. Unlike Libra, the Private Eye doesn't care whether justice is *seen* to be done, nor whether anybody else agrees with his or her idea of justice. To Scorpio, a shot in a dark alley might seem a good solution to a problem.

The only character who is happy to do this job is the Tennis Champion. He can change his focus from open competition to applying his energies and ruthlessness in underground ways.

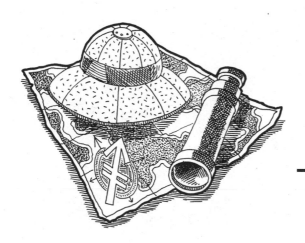

Sagittarius ♐

9th House

Explorer

The Sagittarius job depends first of all on feeling sure of one's place in society, and then going all out to make the most of it. It is like belonging to a good club, which gives you the freedom to do all kinds of things you couldn't do on your own—as long as you stick to the rules.

Images for Sagittarius are being an Explorer, with the resources of a wealthy nation behind the expedition, or a Foreign Correspondent, again with the resources of a big newspaper or television station. The Sagittarius job offers a lot of freedom and responsibility, but it is not the truly freelance freedom and responsibility of Aries. A planet doing the Sagittarius job is always aware that he or she has to report back and get the results the organization expects.

This job is something of a paradox. The Explorer has wide and expansive goals, but is not free to change them at whim. It is something like the Gemini job, except that Sagittarius needs to understand what underlies the facts in a way that Gemini never bothers about.

The Computer Whiz Kid doesn't like this job; there are too many loose ends and gray areas. Favorite Uncle is the one who really enjoys Sagittarius.

♑ Capricorn

10th House

Business Executive

If Sagittarius is about enjoying the freedom of social position, Capricorn is about enjoying the power of it. A planet doing the Capricorn job has to be serious, responsible, and ambitious, enjoying power and responsibility for their own sakes as well as for the material advantages that may go with them.

The high-pressure, successful Business Executive is the image for Capricorn. This is especially true if we think of him or her as someone who has built a career from nothing. "Log cabin to White House" is very Capricorn. The problem for Capricorn is that the Executive has to be on the ball twenty-four hours a day. He or she has to be seen as efficient and in control, so can't afford to relax and goof off. This leads to tension, isolation, and pessimism. The Executive looks, and is, successful, but he or she is working hard all the time to keep it that way.

Capricorn can't afford to take too many risks or act flashy. The Executive has to work by patient, disciplined steps, putting off immediate pleasures for the sake of the long-term goal.

The Old Math Teacher is the best character for this job because he understands the need for work, discipline, and precision. Tennis Champion is good, too, for the same reasons.

Aquarius ♒

11th House

Social Worker

Sagittarius is about enjoying oneself within the system. Capricorn is about using the system as a personal power base. In contrast, Aquarius is concerned with improving the system, perhaps even destroying it if it has become too rigid. A planet doing the Aquarius job has to have a social conscience. He or she has to want the system to work for everybody.

A good image for Aquarius is a Social Worker. The job requirements are to recognize and fight against the injustices of the system. In Aquarius, the character doesn't have to relate personally to the people he or she is helping. In fact, it is better not to because that can interfere with the bigger picture and with fitting everything into the idealistic social theories that Aquarius is so good at. The Social Worker is frequently in the position of championing people he or she doesn't care two cents about—or even can't stand!

It's a fairly schizo sort of job. As theories and policies change, the Social Worker can end up supporting one lot of people one week and a completely different crowd the next.

Again, the Old Math Teacher does this job best. As in Libra, Aquarius brings out the side of him that wants to tie up all the loose ends and make all the equations come out right.

♓ Pisces

12th House

Castaway

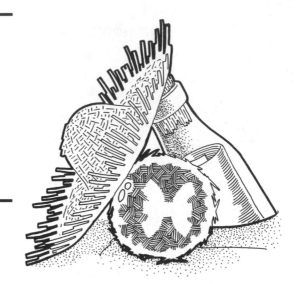

Aquarius was about rebelling against the system or, at least, questioning it. Pisces is about dropping out altogether. In the Pisces job, a planet has to give up material values and goodies, and turn to inner values. In the Pisces job, facts and reason no longer work very well; feelings, intuition, imagination, and compassion are needed now.

In fact, there is no *job* that really fits Pisces. There are situations that work well, such as being in the hospital with depression or marooned on a desert island. The desert island is the one we will use, since we can suppose that it is beautiful and unspoiled, with abundant plant and animal life. It is desert only in the sense of being uninhabited. This will bring out the positive and pleasurable aspects of Pisces, as well as the introversion and loneliness.

Fretting and planning to escape will not work for the Castaway marooned on the island. There is nothing he or she can do to get away. The thing to do is to work with what's there on the island, and to cultivate inner strength and peace. The planet has to learn that, in this situation, sitting for hours in meditation will get better results than building a boat.

Favorite Uncle handles the situation best; he is a philosophical old campaigner. Temple Dancer enjoys it too. It brings out her strong natural and mystical qualities.

Sun in
the Signs
and Houses

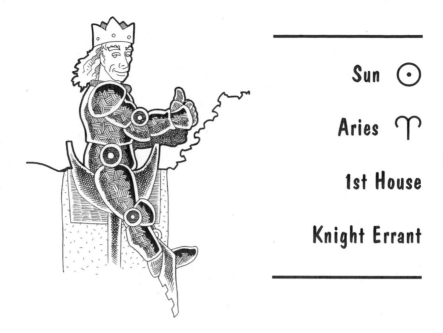

Sun ☉

Aries ♈

1st House

Knight Errant

The King is a Knight Errant. The job suits the King marvelously, especially if he gets to be a *famous* Knight Errant. He loves it all—the danger, the jousting, making a name for himself, rescuing damsels, and battling with evil enchanters. He lives by a strict Code of Honor and would rather be eaten by a dragon than not be true to it. Not that he thinks about it much. All he cares about is being able to feel proud of himself and getting plenty of action.

People with Sun in Aries or First tend to see themselves as pioneers. They always have to be breaking new ground and being *first*. As they charge enthusiastically toward each new goal, they may leave a lot of bodies in their wake, some of them innocent bystanders. Then the Sun in Aries or First wonders why there are people around who seem resentful and jealous. He or she was only following the Code of Honor! These people are not big on tact. They get so locked into achieving their objectives that they don't have time for it, but they are brave and loyal. If they give their word or make a commitment to something, they will move heaven and earth to keep it.

Sun in Aries or First people need to have their achievements recognized, rather like a child saying, "Look what I've done!" They also believe, consciously or secretly, that they really are the best, that nobody else is going to be able to do a job properly. These people are usually poor at delegating. They are liable to take on too much and become stressed and exhausted, though they have great powers of recovery.

⊙ **Sun**

♉ **Taurus**

2nd House

Farmer

The King has to earn his living as a Farmer, let's say a big landowner working his own estates. There is no scope for heroics, no fanfares and combats. The King has to work with the processes of nature, fit in with times and seasons, planting and harvesting, and getting up at dawn to milk the cows. It is not too bad a job for the King because he can take pride in his farm, but there is no place for ego and charisma so he feels somewhat frustrated. He has to be King, and therefore the best, whatever he does, so he will become obsessed with his routines and with his property.

People with Sun in Taurus or Second will be concerned with patience, taking pains, doing things slowly and properly. They usually like possessions and dislike being separated from them. People with Sun in Taurus or Second enjoy stability. They hate change of any kind, especially unexpected change. Even when the change has been planned for and thought out well in advance, they are not all that happy about it.

Suns in Taurus or Second have a great need to have their feet on the ground, money in their pockets, and enthusiastic partners in their beds. They can be stupefyingly stubborn and conservative, stuck in their routines to a degree that drives other people crazy, but these people are reliable and tough; they usually outlast their critics and enemies.

The King has a job as a News Reporter. The work is a little menial for him. He doesn't much like the people he has to work with or the stories he has to chase. Still, if he has to do the job, he will be the best. It brings out the performer in him rather than the leader. He soon learns how to be pushy and inquisitive, and to act as if the story he is following is the most important thing in the world. He puts on a good show, but he secretly rather despises the triviality of it all.

Sun in Gemini or Third people will be restless and curious about everything, unable to sit still. They will often give the impression of being in overdrive, with a dozen things that must be done at once, disorganized, yet somehow finding the energy to juggle the incredible load of activities they take on. There is usually an element of pride at being able to handle such demands, however much the person may complain.

Suns in Gemini or Third must be able to feel that they are in the know about everything that is going on. They feel they will die if they don't have the latest gossip. They need to listen to all the news bulletins, and endlessly discuss and rehash events with all of their friends. They don't so much live their lives as act out a life style. At their worst, Suns in Gemini or Third can be merely noisy and superficial. They often seem worried, but little of the vast amount of information they acquire really affects them.

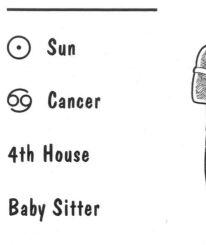

⊙ **Sun**

♋ **Cancer**

4th House

Baby Sitter

The King is acting as a Baby Sitter. This is a rotten job for him because the baby's needs must come first. The baby is the center of attention, and for the King, that is almost as bad as being deposed! Somehow, he will contrive to express his personality and get his own way. How is he going to be the monarch and, at the same time, devote himself to caring for another person? Answer: He will be *better* at knowing about babies and looking after them than anyone else. He'll also do the caring on his own schedule as far as he can.

Sun in Cancer or Fourth people will have a feeling of rather worrying responsibility, as if they know they ought to be doing something but can't quite remember what it is. This makes them a little distracted, edgy, and suspicious, rather touchy, and quick to imagine that they are being got at.

Above all, Sun in Cancer or Fourth people need to feel that everything in the environment is organized, every emergency foreseen and forestalled. This is often at the root of their well-known concern for others. The concern is genuine enough, but mainly because having something ailing around them makes Sun in Cancer or Fourth feel bad. It's like the critic said about a performance of King Lear—in Cancer, the Sun plays the King as if he expected someone else to play the Ace—he's nervous, diffident, and not at all royal.

The King is now a highly charismatic Pop Star. He loves the job and gives it a hundred percent, and then some more. There he is, in the spotlight, wearing some flashy and bizarre costume, belting out a number with all the emotional power he has. The audience is mesmerized by it. He uses the music, the lights, and the drama to beam out love, life, and sexuality to the audience, and they beam it back to him ten times over.

People with Sun in Leo or Fifth will have the feeling that they *ought* to be larger than life, even if they are not. They need to be able to feel proud of themselves, convinced that they are doing something big, worthwhile, and important. Every Sun in Leo person knows that their true place is in the spotlight. The problem is that it's often the devil of a job to get there! So they can be very dramatic, even melodramatic, taking rather absurd stands on matters of pride and honor. Truth is, the Sun in Leo or Fifth person is often a little old-fashioned, an anachronism.

These people need constant feedback and applause, but in real life, there aren't that many opportunities for adulation! There is an awful tendency for Sun in Leo or Fifth to withdraw into their own majesty, swishing their tails in the consciousness of their own superiority. At their worst, they can be insufferably arrogant and patronizing. Or, at their very worst, boring, insisting on doing their acts long after the customers have gone home or gone to sleep.

Sun

♍ **Virgo**

6th House

Doctor

Now the King is a Doctor, remote and professional, doing everything by the book. He is supposed to stick to the facts, remain detached, and not let messy human feelings get in his way. It is not a good job for the King. He has to suppress most of his real nature, though he can boss his patients around quite a lot and so work off some of his leadership qualities. There's not much satisfaction in that because he is still hiding behind his "doctor" mask, not being himself.

People with Sun in Virgo or Sixth feel above all that they have to be useful. They have to fix things, be responsible, put work before pleasure. In fact, the very concept of pleasure is not one that they can easily relate to. They can be workaholics, feeling that they are never really off duty. They are driven by obscure guilt to take all the burdens of the world on their backs.

Sun in Virgo or Sixth has a great need to be right. Someone said that human beings would rather be right than be happy, and this is true in spades of the Sun in Virgo or Sixth person. They often have a curious mixture of modesty and superiority. They take pride in how modest and professional they are. They are the ones who cut the crap and get on with the job; but if they feel they have not done the job, their self-esteem collapses completely. At their worst, they can be critical bores, analyzing everything to death.

The King is refereeing a boxing match. This is the worst job he has had yet. All the attention is on the contestants. They both hate him. The crowd hates him. Everything he does is wrong; he is merely a necessary evil! About all he can do to express his majesty is to be better at being fair and impartial than anyone else.

People with Sun in Libra or Seventh find it difficult to take sides or form a definite view about anything. Left to themselves, they will sit on the fence forever; but they are seldom left to themselves. People make demands on them, and they go along with these demands, often to the point where they begin to feel resentful. Then they react and their friends can't understand why they are suddenly being so difficult, but they are just restoring the balance.

Sun in Libra or Seventh people must have balance and harmony in their lives. This is their great need. If they try to be definite and assertive, others misunderstand them and they get more kicks than rewards. A way of getting around this is to form alliances and relationships. On the other hand, dealing with actual relationships is often messy and distressing. It's hard for Sun in Libra or Seventh people to win. They try to keep everything on the level of charm, courtesy, and good manners. Passion is not welcome. At their worst, they are elusive, indecisive, and downright unreliable. In Lord Byron's words, "[He] had turned his coat and would have turned his skin."

☉ Sun

♏ Scorpio

8th House

Private Eye

The King is working as a Private Eye. The job offends his royal nature. It disgusts him to have to intrude into other people's lives, risk his neck, rub shoulders with gangsters, deal with dead bodies, and sift through garbage cans. All this gets him very angry. He is determined to solve all his cases and make sure the culprits *pay* for their crimes.

People with Sun in Scorpio or Eighth live in a state of mild shock, as though they know something that other people don't and wish they didn't. They know that life is rough, tough, and mean. The knowledge may not be very conscious, but it is there. Suns in Scorpio or Eighth take nothing at face value. They are reserved and suspicious.

The big need of these people is to keep their dark secrets. They rarely open up. This is partly because they are scared of being betrayed, partly because they are keeping score. They have a long memory for slights and injuries, real or imagined. At their worst, Suns in Scorpio or Eighth can be ruthless, vengeful, and inhuman. Whoever said "Revenge is a dish best eaten cold" probably had Sun in Scorpio or Eighth.

Sun ☉

Sagittarius ♐

9th House

Explorer

Now the King is an Explorer. He is an old-fashioned one, like a nineteenth-century Englishman exploring Africa with a few bearers and his own courage. This job is not quite what the King likes best, but it is a breath of fresh air after the last three. After all, he is extending the Empire and bringing the benefits of civilization to the benighted natives! He can't fully be himself because he has to be a team player to a large extent. In the end, he has to report back to the organization that financed his expedition.

People with Sun in Sagittarius or Ninth are adventurous, either physically or mentally, but at the same time, they need to play by the rules. They are rather like Sun in Gemini or Third, but with much more depth and much more passionate commitment. "Gung ho" is probably the keyword for these people. There is no real individuality about their enthusiasm, more that they are able to get genuinely excited by the values of the group.

The great need of Sun in Sagittarius or Ninth is to be socially accepted and to be recognized as a valuable member of the team or club. Usually, this means that they have a breezy and cheerful, "Let's have a party!" approach to life. At their worst, though, they can be grim fanatics, wanting to force everyone into their own beliefs.

☉ **Sun**

♑ **Capricorn**

10th House

Business Executive

The King is a high-powered, high-pressure Business Executive. At first glance, you might think the job would suit him, but it doesn't. He's not really his own master, as he has to answer to the shareholders, and he despises the wheeling and dealing, the manipulating and infighting he has to do. He values loyalty more than efficiency and will keep loyal workers on when he should fire them. He himself becomes less than efficient and inclined to be cynical and dour.

People with Sun in Capricorn or Tenth will experience a lot of pressure to achieve. They tend to be very impressed by "authority" even after they become authorities themselves. They are always status conscious, concerned about what the neighbors will think. Suns in Capricorn or Tenth can't stand failure or mistakes, either in others or in themselves. They have to be perfect, and they spend a lot of time and energy in *looking* perfect.

The great need of these people is to fit in to what everyone else believes and then dominate by fitting in better than the others. They have a compulsion to succeed, but secretly believe they can't win. Still, they go all out to win, or fall down trying, and their determination generally brings them a good deal of success. At their worst, Suns in Capricorn or Tenth are selfish and ruthless users of other people, taking all they can get from their friends and trashing them when they are of no further use.

Sun ☉

Aquarius ≈

11th House

Social Worker

The King is a Social Worker. This is the worst job of all for him. He doesn't believe in social work; he believes in paternal benevolence, centered on himself. He has to work at a distance from the people he is concerned with, seeing them as case histories rather than as human beings to be charmed and inspired by his presence. When he meets his cases, he doesn't usually like them very much. He becomes efficient, but unfeeling and cold. He gets none of the praise, love, and feedback he craves, only more demands on his energies.

People with Sun in Aquarius or Eleventh have an underlying feeling of being disoriented. They believe, or want to believe, or think they should believe, that everyone is equal. Trouble is, they don't feel equal. They are often bright and perceptive, full of unusual ways of seeing things. They feel a bit special, then feel guilty about feeling special.

Above all, Suns in Aquarius or Eleventh need to be seen as socially conscious, liberal, yet independent and detached. They often have an edgy, electric quality that attracts others, yet at the same time keeps them at a distance. They tend to have lots of acquaintances, but few, if any, close friends. They talk a lot about "commitment," but hate to be committed. At their worst, Suns in Aquarius or Eleventh can be incredibly stubborn and self-contradictory. They can argue a point with total conviction one day and exactly the opposite view the next, with equally schizy conviction!

⊙ Sun

♓ Pisces

12th House

Castaway

The King is a Desert Island Castaway. At least he can spin his fantasies of being king of all he surveys; but you can't be much of a king on a desert island, and he misses his true calling. He gets very depressed and spends a lot of time walking up and down the beach, hoping to be rescued. He periodically convinces himself he will be, then slumps into despair.

People with Sun in Pisces or Twelfth feel rather isolated, as if they were living in a bubble. Yet, at the same time, they also have a poor sense of boundaries, not knowing whether the thoughts and feelings they have are their own or belong to somebody else. They often have a hard time knowing fact from fantasy. Suns in Pisces or Twelfth are open to all possibilities and experiences. This can be very charming or very irritating to other people. Their big problem is their tendency to feel and act martyred.

The great need of Sun in Pisces or Twelfth is to find some inner strength or inspiration, otherwise they are lost, bewildered, and ineffective. Also, without some inner touchstone, they can be gullible, easily molded by stronger-minded people. The plus side of all this is that they can be highly compassionate and understanding. At their worst, Suns in Pisces or Twelfth can be poor fish indeed, always moaning and complaining about what a bad time they are having.

Moon in
the Signs
and Houses

Moon ☽

Aries ♈

1st House

Knight Errant

Some bizarre circumstance has compelled the Housekeeper to put on armor and ride about the countryside looking for battles and adventures. She hates the job, being a gentle person, happy with her home and routines. Though she can be fiercely protective, ready to attack anything that threatens her or her home and family, it is not her nature to go looking for trouble. Still, she is very adaptable and able to call on her aggressive instincts. Though the Code of Honor seems pretty silly to her, she can abide by it. She acts so brave that all the other knights are frightened of her. They never realize she is a woman, though she is scared all the time.

People with Moon in Aries or First always feel under pressure. Everything is an emergency and there is no leisure for gracious living. These people are highly enthusiastic, but seldom tactful. They make snap judgments and are not very tolerant of anything outside their usual sphere. They can't stand to be criticized or even told anything because it feels too much like an attack, and they have enough of that already. Moon in Aries or First people can be very moody, but they move so fast and come on so strong you don't notice their moods. They expect you to, though!

These people are always proving something to themselves. Action is what counts, especially being *seen* to be active and competitive. Sometimes, Moon in Aries or First people feel so insecure they will do something stupidly reckless to prove how brave they are. Russian roulette was probably invented by one of them.

☽ Moon

♉ Taurus

2nd House

Farmer

For the Housekeeper, running an old-fashioned farm is right up her street. It's not so different from her real job, not in essentials, anyway. Doing the routine chores of a farm, being attuned to the processes of nature, looking after growing things, all come easily to the Housekeeper and she is very happy doing this job. The only problem with it is that she gets too locked in to her routines and her horizons become narrow.

People with Moon in Taurus or Second are likely to be solid, not to say stolid! Taurus is, of course, the Bull, and these people can be as hard to rouse as a peaceful bull or as difficult to deflect as a charging one. Obstinacy and persistence are their middle names. In truth, they just don't feel good about themselves unless they have a secure, stable environment and routines. Normally placid, they can go wild if their security is threatened.

Moon in Taurus or Second people like to feel their feet on the ground in all sorts of ways. Every experience or idea has to be put to some practical use or, at least, fitted into some overall scheme. Although they have very strong emotional and sexual natures, they are not usually very demonstrative. Their need to have everything under control tends to keep them inhibited. The same goes for money. They don't normally have much trouble in making money or managing it, but they can be cautious about spending it. The Moon in Taurus or Second can look much like the Sun. The difference is internal. The King in this job is earthy and possessive because he is over-compensating. The Housekeeper is that way because she enjoys it.

Moon ☽
Gemini ♊
3rd House
News Reporter

The Housekeeper *hates* being a News Reporter. Yelling into the phone in a busy news room, chasing stories, meeting deadlines, are all absolutely wrong for her quiet and peaceful nature. It's worse than being a Knight Errant. In that job, she can at least concentrate on one thing at a time. As a reporter, she is constantly torn into a dozen pieces. She soon begins relying on aspirins and tranquilizers to numb her feelings and hold herself together. She gets the job done, though she is living on her nerves all the time.

People with Moon in Gemini or Third are often like firecrackers, bouncing from one thing to another. Feelings are generally well-suppressed. These people may well *talk* about their feelings and inner states, but they are not really connected with them. Because of this, some Moons in Gemini or Third can be astonishingly unpredictable and inconsiderate. Although they seem to be so interested in other people and all kinds of things, what they are really interested in is themselves and their ideas. They are often compulsive print addicts, reading the corn flakes package if there is nothing else.

The Moon is the security function and, in Gemini or Third, she is overloaded with stimuli. Moon in Gemini or Third people have a poor sense of security. A lot of their fast talking and hyperactivity is a way of keeping busy so they don't have time to notice how precarious they feel. There are some Moon in Gemini or Third people who are unexpectedly taciturn. They usually make up for it by being full of schemes of one sort or another, or always doing little jobs about the house.

) **Moon**

69 **Cancer**

4th House

Baby Sitter

Being a Baby Sitter is a marvelous job for the Housekeeper. The strong mothering, nurturing, organizing instinct she has is exactly what the job requires. Cuddling the baby, ensuring that she is warm, clean, and properly fed, uttering kootchy-kootchy-koo noises at her, make the Housekeeper glow like a two-hundred-watt bulb. On the other hand, if anything goes wrong, or merely seems likely to go wrong, she will feel guilty, alarmed, and defensive. As with the Taurus job, the Housekeeper's horizons are apt to become very narrow in this one.

Moon in Cancer or Fourth people are usually sympathetic and caring, but with a strong sense of territory. It's as if they live inside a security fence with very sensitive alarms. Do or say the wrong thing and you are out before you know what's happened. Once safely inside, you can get away with a lot. If something goes wrong in your life, your Moon in Cancer or Fourth friend may come halfway across the country to hold your hand.

The catch is that once you're inside the fence, it's hard to get out again. These people will do anything for you, but they also expect you to do anything for them. Above all, they expect you never to *leave* them. Their great problem is that they are much too sensitive to moods, both their own and other people's, so they feel safer dwelling in the past, which doesn't change.

Moon ☽

Leo ♌

5th House

Pop Star

It's amateur night at the local bar. The Housekeeper isn't really cut out to be a Pop Star, but she gets up and has a go at it. Her diffidence shows, though. Her dress and makeup are a little too weird and flashy, she tries too hard to be emotional and dramatic, and she hits a lot of wrong notes. Actually, she has had a couple of drinks too many or she wouldn't be doing it at all. *She* thinks she is giving a stunning performance and doesn't notice the audience wincing.

People with Moon in Leo or Fifth usually have some of this overstated theatricality. They seem to feel they have to be this way, to be seen as warm, generous, and enthusiastic about life, but it doesn't quite come across. They are too busy performing to notice and learn from other people's reactions to the performance. It's no good drawing their attention to their flaws. They will either be very hurt or dismiss your comments as jealousy, or, even more likely, simply not understand what you're saying.

Moon in Leo or Fifth people often seem to have a sense of being onto a good thing. Life looks rosy and they are prepared to enjoy it, letting the pieces fall where they may. It's as if the Moon has stopped being the mother and is having a turn at being the child. These people are highly egocentric, but normally entirely without malice. They see life as a marvelous game to be played, or drama to be enjoyed, and they just want to get on with it.

☽ Moon

♍ Virgo

6th House

Doctor

Being a Doctor suits the Housekeeper's need to look after people. The problem is, she would rather do that in a feeling way and, in this job, she can't. She has to be objective, analytical, and intellectual, and she is not strong on those qualities. She loves seeing patients and writing prescriptions, but the vast amount of knowledge and paperwork she has to keep up with wears her down. It's the same problem she had in Gemini, though there are more compensations in this job; but denying her sympathies and feelings, working with facts and figures, makes her a bit scratchy. She is liable to become a worrier, a fusspot, and a nag.

People with Moon in Virgo or Sixth tend to see the world as being full of problems. Life seems like some kind of intelligence test they are not doing very well on. They never really feel they have done a job to the best of their ability, even when they have. They don't sleep well, and are never certain that they have locked the door or turned off the gas. They are liable to feel victimized by "the system."

Some Moons in Virgo or Sixth can suppress the wired-up tension and act relaxed and casual. The tension then comes out as minor health problems. In theory, Moons in Virgo or Sixth should enjoy doing housework and keeping their places spic-and-span. In practice, it often gets to be too much. They let everything go and then feel guilty for living in a mess. But there is also a kind of Moon in Virgo or Sixth that, like Moon in Gemini or Third, never stops running. The motive is the same—so they won't have to stop and think about what it all means.

The Housekeeper is some kind of Judge or Referee or, perhaps, a Party Hostess, some job where she has to be fair and impartial. This doesn't suit her very well because she prefers to play favorites. The people she loves are okay, and should be helped as much as possible. The people she does not love are jerks, and should be kept down by any means, foul or fair. She can't do the job if she follows her feelings, so she develops a bright, efficient social manner.

People with Moon in Libra or Seventh don't necessarily have a bright social manner. They can be quite gruff and reserved, but they are always watching points. They always have the feeling that some kind of balance has to be maintained. This usually comes out as politeness and insisting on observing etiquette and small ceremonies. Spontaneous they are not, though some of them may *act* spontaneous. Because of the suppressed feelings, Moons in Libra or Seventh can be very intuitive or psychic. Some of them merely imagine that they are, mistake their fantasies for facts, and act on them rather disastrously.

Moons in Libra or Seventh are usually good at giving compliments and like to get them in return. They can be very flattering and attentive. They are rather inclined to store up real or imagined injustices, annoyances, and resentments. When they have enough of these, they will cash them in by doing something irrational and inappropriate, like getting drunk and insulting everyone at the office party—all without guilt or remorse—they are merely restoring the balance.

Moon in the Signs and Houses   63

☽ Moon

♏ Scorpio

8th House

Private Eye

The Housekeeper is good at being a Private Eye. That is, she is good at the job, though the job isn't good for her. She can use her intuitive and psychic powers to the full and knows who committed the crime long before she can prove it by logic and evidence. She solves most of her cases one way or another, and never forgets a detail of any of them. What she hates is all the mean people she has to deal with and all the mean things she has to do herself to get the better of them. Suspicion and distrust become her way of life, and this warps her real nature.

Moon in Scorpio or Eighth people have some touch of paranoia. Somewhere, in the backs of their minds, is an uneasy feeling that they have done something wrong and are liable to be found out. The sort of irrational twinge of guilt that most us are liable to get when we pass a police officer on the street haunts Moon in Scorpio or Eighth all the time. So they are very interested in control of themselves and their environment.

The impression they usually create is one of blocked energy. They want to know all about you but don't tell you much about themselves in return. The element of constant control makes them very tough and they are great survivors.

As with Sun and Moon in Taurus, the difference between Sun and Moon in Scorpio is more at the internal level. The King is angry about being a Private Eye. The Housekeeper is traumatized by it.

Moon ☽

Sagittarius ♐

9th House

Explorer

The Housekeeper is an Explorer, tracking through the jungle with a few bearers to open up a new country. She has to keep on the move, camp out, and look as though she knows what she's doing to hold her party together. It is all a long way from her real concerns. It is hard and dangerous work, but she has committed herself to it. She has geared herself up to meet the challenges of the job, but it is mostly her sense of responsibility for her companions that keeps her going. She may make it, or she may get so homesick that she has a nervous breakdown.

People with Moon in Sagittarius or Ninth enjoy exploring or traveling, either physically or in the mind. They are optimistic, able to meet all challenges, and they give themselves pep talks that really work. They also usually have a powerful conviction of being right, which comes from their need to repress the more intimate feelings. They pursue the goals they have set themselves with great zest. It is rather like dancing on a tightrope. If they stopped to look into the abyss of their feelings, they would probably fall off. Judy Garland had Moon in Sagittarius. She is a rather extreme example of the syndrome of frantic activity leading to breakdown that often seems to happen with this Moon, which is probably the most emotionally repressed of the lot.

Moons in Sagittarius or Ninth can *seem* unconventional, but it is more like burning the candle at both ends than radical thinking. They are tolerant, but only as long as none of their basic assumptions are questioned.

Moon in the Signs and Houses   65

☽ Moon

♑ Capricorn

10th House

Business Executive

Being a high-powered Executive is an awful job for the Housekeeper; the very worst, in fact. Her whole nature is inclined to personal relationships and organic values. Now she has to forget all that and think only of material success, balance sheets, and profit and loss. Libra was bad enough, when she had to be impartial and not favor her friends. In Capricorn, she may well have to fire her friends and promote people she can't stand, for the good of the job. The Housekeeper loses her real nature entirely and becomes a hard shell of herself.

People with Moon in Capricorn often seem to have a deep and angry sense of having been denied or cheated of something essential to a life worth living. They compensate by taking a very pragmatic, ruthless, ambitious, and often mercenary view of life. Hitler is an extreme and notorious example. They live by the law of the jungle, expecting other people automatically to be competitors who have to be beaten, tricked, charmed, or manipulated into submission. This creates great alienation, and every now and then, Moons in Capricorn seem to engineer some comeuppance or disaster for themselves, which they need to see as a learning experience. Deep down, they believe themselves to be unlovable, and this casts a cold, heavy shadow on everything else.

Moon in the Tenth House seems to be an exception to the rule that the house is like the sign, only more so. Moons in the Tenth *are* ambitious, hard working, and out for number one, but they don't seem as relentless about it, nor as good at it, as their Capricorn cousins.

Moon ☽

Aquarius ≈≈

11th House

Social Worker

Being a Social Worker is a little better for the Housekeeper than the last job, but not much. At least she is dealing with people's needs and human situations again. But she can't relate to her clients in the fully personal way that is her real nature. She has to work with the regulations and deal with more clients than she has proper time and energy for. So she is still frustrated, having to work with people at arm's length. She can't use her intuition and feelings, but has to go by theories and bureaucratic precedents.

People with Moon in Aquarius or Eleventh usually give the impression of being not quite with you. They often have a kind of puzzled need to work everything out and make it fit into their own preconceived schemes. If they can't find good reasons or justifications for their feelings, they will deny the feelings. It's not so much that these people are rational as that they consider that they *ought* to be rational. A spiritual teacher has said that life is a mystery to be lived, not a problem to be solved. Moon in Aquarius or Eleventh wouldn't agree with that at all. For many of these people, life is like a Rubik's cube, which they are forever twisting into new combinations and never getting right.

They set great store by friendships as long as they don't have to be emotionally committed. Possibly because of the fear of commitment, many of them seem to have split personalities. They can argue vigorously for a point of view one day and equally powerfully for its opposite the next day, or even in a few hours.

☽ Moon

♓ Pisces

12th House

Castaway

At last, the Housekeeper is in a situation where she can relax and restore her shattered nerves after the tension of the last few jobs. Being a Castaway on a desert island brings out the witchy, magical side of her. She soon develops a sense of community with all the wildlife on the island, and she loves to walk in the foam on the beach. Just being near the ocean gives her a tremendous boost. She is sad at having no humans to care about, but she doesn't dwell on that too much. Most of the time, she enjoys the solitude, but on bad days she feels unbearably lonely.

People with Moon in Pisces or Twelfth House need a lot of time to themselves. They don't relate very well to the rough and tumble of the world, and they need to keep some part of themselves well separated from it, otherwise they quickly get drained, exhausted, and depressed. They are very sensitive to other people's feelings—indeed, *anything's* feelings. They will rescue a spider from the bath rather than kill it, even if they hate spiders. There is, however, a variety of Moon in Pisces or Twelfth that will overcompensate for this sensitivity and outwardly act just the opposite. One Moon in Pisces, Aleister Crowley, was a big game hunter, yet still squeamish in many ways. They can also act in an outrageously individualistic manner, as if they don't care a damn what others think of them (Crowley again).

Moons in Pisces or Twelfth are basically kind and considerate, though often their judgment is poor and they are liable to get ripped off. Some of them develop a cautious and even miserly attitude in self-protection.

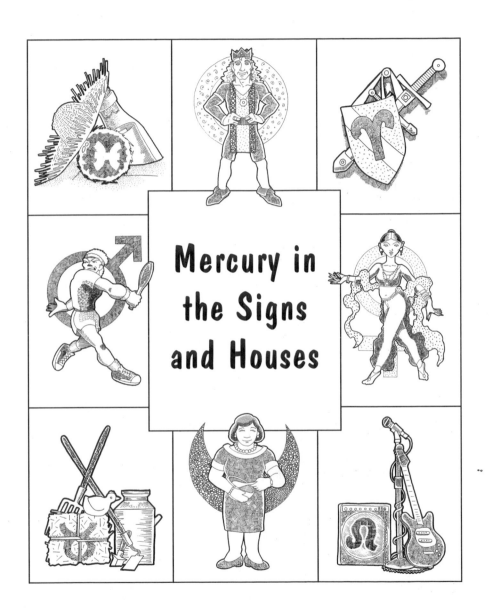

Mercury in the Signs and Houses

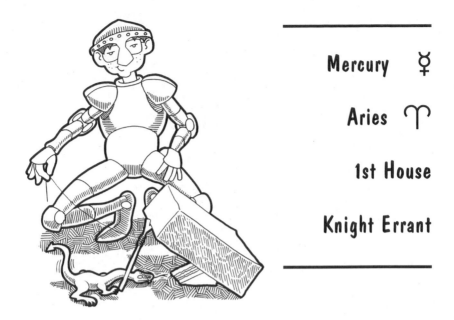

Mercury ☿

Aries ♈

1st House

Knight Errant

Computer Whiz Kid hasn't got the brute strength and reckless courage to be a good Knight Errant. He has to be a sneaky Knight Errant. Maybe he paints a skull on his shield to make himself look more fearsome or connects his lance to a power pack to electrocute his opponent. He is not above strewing pebbles on the ground so that his opponent's horse will stumble. It is all a game to him; he is not really involved.

People with Mercury in Aries or First are always figuring angles, working out new ways to win. They tend to speak and think very quickly and will always be a jump ahead of anyone else. Mercuries in Aries or First weave such a strong defensive net of words, opinions, and attitudes that you can't get past it. They love a debate, but it is just an exercise to strengthen their own point of view.

Mercuries in Aries or First think that all their problems will be solved if only they can get enough information. Plans, goals, and flowcharts are meat and drink to these people, and they are full of schemes for making money and making their relationships work. They love books of the positive thinking kind, but they never learn anything from them because they are totally unwilling to change.

☿ Mercury

♉ Taurus

2nd House

Farmer

Being a Farmer is a real drag for the Computer Whiz Kid. It's all too earthy and inconvenient. He doesn't *want* to be in touch with the earth and natural rhythms. He wants to impose his own ideas on everything and, of course, that doesn't work on a farm, or only to a limited extent. Stuck in this job, the Whiz Kid becomes baffled and sulky. He has so little opportunity to use his intellectual powers that they wither away. All he can talk about is chicken runs and pig food.

This doesn't mean that people with Mercury in Taurus or Second aren't bright. They may be very bright indeed, but to get them to look at anything from a new angle is almost impossible. They *must* see concrete results from what they are doing and they pride themselves on being realistic and practical. They miss a lot of things because they can't see beyond the values of the street and the marketplace.

They can also be very heavy and serious. Typical, in this respect, is Freud, with Mercury in Taurus, who wrote a laborious and boring analysis of humor! His reducing everything to sex is also a good example of the overdone materialism of this Mercury placing. Though these people tend to overdo being practical, they do get on with the job. You can rely on them to see ways of doing things and solving problems, at least within their limits.

Mercury ☿

Gemini ⚄

3rd House

News Reporter

Being a News Reporter is marvelous for the Computer Whiz Kid. He doesn't have to get emotionally involved and he is actually being paid for running about like a bluetailed fly and sticking his nose into anything and everything. He carries a laptop computer and mobile telephone everywhere he goes, so he always has access to information and is always in touch. This is the job the Whiz Kid does best, and he is happy to do it all day long.

People with Mercury in Gemini or Third above all want to *know* things. They are often surprisingly earnest and don't seem to have much sense of humor. Their strong focus on asking questions and gathering information tends to make them serious in a paradoxical way, like butterflies on a tight schedule. In many ways, "paradox" is a keyword for Mercury in Gemini or Third. Unkind people might say "schizo." They are often witty, but seldom funny.

Mercuries in Gemini or Third are not necessarily fast, live-wire talkers. They seem to fall into two types, as you might expect with anything to do with Gemini—the Chatterbox and the Lecturer. The Chatterbox talks a lot but doesn't know much. The Lecturer can be quite taciturn, but he knows a lot, and once he does start talking, spares you very little of what he knows. With either type, the supreme cruelty is preventing them from watching the news on television.

☿ **Mercury**

♋ **Cancer**

4th House

Baby Sitter

Baby sitting is another job the Computer Whiz Kid is useless at. He is embarrassed by babies and has absolutely no feeling for their needs. He has to have a detailed list of instructions. If something goes wrong and he can't find the answer in his instructions, he will probably panic. In fact, he'll probably panic as his response of choice in any event! To try to keep on top of the job, he may write a book—a manual of baby sitting that keeps everything safely theoretical.

People with Mercury in Cancer or Fourth feel more or less permanently challenged by things they can't quite get a grip on. These people feel that, if only they could *understand*—especially anything to do with emotions— they would cope well enough. They create huge thought systems of one kind or another, trying to pigeonhole every fact in the universe so that it can't leap up and bite them. They have to have explanations for everything, and they frequently have an air of preoccupied defensive-ness, like the Computer Whiz Kid wondering what the hell the baby is going to do next.

There are three famous Mercuries in Cancer who show the syndrome well. There is Alexandre Dumas, who wrote vast historical novels; Marcel Proust, who wrote a huge novel about detailed memories; and Carl Jung, who constructed a vast, detailed system of psychology based mostly on the influence of the past. In general, Mercury in Cancer or Fourth will be much concerned with memories, maintaining links with the past, and keeping up with old friends.

Mercury ☿

Leo ♌

5th House

Pop Star

Computer Whiz Kid is too cerebral to be a Pop Star, so he doesn't even try. He might croak through a song in a flat, Bob Dylanish way, then he'll stand at the mike and tell intellectual, sophisticated gags—great one-liners. A sixteen-year-old Woody Allen doing a standup routine is pretty much the picture. Computer Whiz Kid gets a lot of laughs, and it goes to his head, making him think he knows a lot more than he does. In fact, he's all timing and technique, and no heart.

People with Mercury in Leo or Fifth usually take themselves very seriously. They strike dramatic attitudes and expect to get their own way. Some of them are very good at "stepping backwards into the limelight," as someone said of Lawrence of Arabia, who had Mercury in Leo. They can say and do things that look self-deprecating, but they end up in the spotlight just the same.

The way Mercury in Leo or Fifth people communicate is usually enthusiastic. Even though they may be talking about how depressed they are and how terrible life is, they'll do it in an enthusiastic, interesting, and dramatic manner. Some of them have a variant of this manner, which is to be so terribly jaded and sophisticated, my dear, that they can hardly be bothered to speak at all. There's as much attention-getting drama in this mode as the other; it's just a little more subtle. They are all dogmatic. They have strong opinions on everything, and they'd die sooner than be wrong about any of them.

☿ Mercury

♍ Virgo

6th House

Doctor

As a Doctor, Computer Whiz Kid is in his element, and for the reasons the Housekeeper wasn't. He loves the tremendous store of facts he has to keep on top of. He even enjoys the paperwork. He has no feeling at all for his patients as people, but he knows what's good for them. As long as the complaints his patients bring to him are straightforward physical things, he is an excellent Doctor. If he has to cope with someone who has depression or some psychosomatic ailment, he feels threatened and becomes difficult and unhelpful.

Mercuries in Virgo or Sixth work hard, commit themselves totally to the things they do, and see themselves as professional. If you want to flatter someone with Mercury in Virgo or Sixth, tell them they are professional, competent, and down-to-earth. They may only grunt an acknowledgment, but your words will keep their self-esteem going for days!

Self-esteem is always precarious with these people. If they get into something that isn't covered by their coping techniques, they are in trouble. It's very hard for Mercury in Virgo or Sixth to ask for help. After all, they are supposed to be the professionals with all the answers.

"Cope" is another Mercury in Virgo or Sixth word, but they are poor at organizing their lives, especially their emotional lives. They get locked into a narrow point of view. These people do have a basic flexibility, but they may have to spend years doing the wrong things before they discover it.

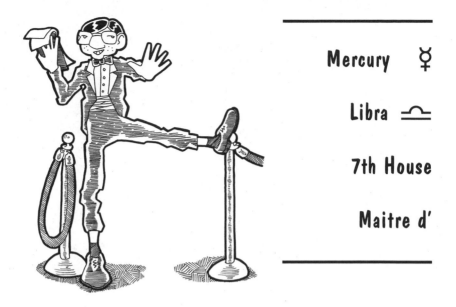

Being Maitre d' of a classy restaurant is not a bad job for the Computer Whiz Kid, though he's a bit gauche and overeager. What he lacks in tact and smoothness, he makes up for in being smart. He's good at handling all the details. He has mnemonic lists to help him remember everyone's name and preferences so he can make them feel good and ensure they get their favorite food cooked and served just right. He sees himself as a fixer, and what counts for him is both what you know and who you know.

People with Mercury in Libra or Seventh will do everything they can to keep everybody happy. They are the ones who buy all those books on how to win friends and influence people. They prefer to keep things light and they come on as great optimists. This is not so much because they really *are* optimistic, but because they see optimism as being the right attitude.

They are almost always agreeable and friendly. There is a variety of Mercury in Libra or Seventh that feels strong enough to impose harmony rather than juggle for it as most of them do. This type has long ago made up its mind about everything. Even when they are laying down the law, though, they do it with a powerful air of being fair and reasonable. People with Mercury in Libra or Seventh are almost always at least impressive, and often charismatic. They don't think their ideas through as much as they should, but usually succeed in selling them to others.

☿ Mercury

♏ Scorpio

8th House

Private Eye

Computer Whiz Kid would be a fine Private Eye if he could sit in an armchair and do it all by logic and reason. As it is, he has to go out and deal with all the messy, emotional, and seamy side of life that his clients bring to him. This disgusts him and screws him up, and he gets to the point where he doesn't think and reason very well. After finding out once or twice that his wide-eyed, innocent, and virtuous clients have lied to him, he becomes pathologically suspicious.

People with Mercury in Scorpio or Eighth have the feeling of lost innocence, of knowing something they are not supposed to know. At the same time, they have a compulsion to keep probing, turning over stones that might be better left alone. This is a menace in relationships because they can't resist picking at the little white lies, evasions, and secrets that all relationships need to survive.

These people often have rich and strange inner lives and are more at home with imagination and fantasy than with the real world. William Blake and Aleister Crowley are two famous Mercuries in Scorpio. Both had the faculty of digging deep into the unconscious and producing some remarkable and often incomprehensible writings.

Mercury in Scorpio or Eighth people usually have an air of great intensity and preoccupation. It's rather like Mercury in Cancer or Fourth, but not as puzzled and defensive. It's more that of having a difficult and not very pleasant job to do.

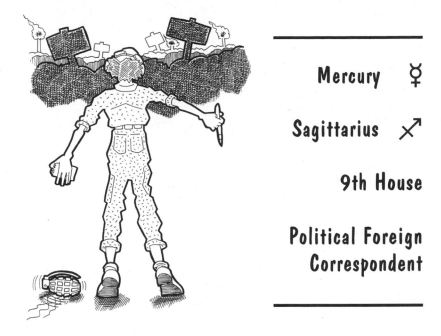

Mercury ☿

Sagittarius ♐

9th House

Political Foreign Correspondent

Let's say Computer Whiz Kid is a Political Foreign Correspondent. This brings up some of the issues better than the Explorer. You might think he would be good at chasing stories, and so he is, up to a point.

However, to do the job really well, he needs to be aware of the big picture and the deeper implications of what he is reporting. This is not his strong point because he is too focused on immediate detail. In this job, the Whiz Kid can be like the Reporter who was sent to cover a boxing match and who came back saying, "There's no story. The champ dropped dead before the fight."

People with Mercury in Sagittarius or Ninth are typically alert and enthusiastic. They take up new ideas and new enterprises in the belief that, this time, they will make the big killing. They rarely do because there is always some element they have not reckoned on, or something they don't know that they think they do know.

That doesn't mean that Mercury in Sagittarius or Ninth can't be successful. Beethoven and Paul Getty are two famous examples of career success, but neither was able to carry much of it over into their private lives. Both were pretty morose as well, which seems against the general tendency of Mercury in Sagittarius or Ninth to be brisk and cheerful. The key, I think, is that these people always feel they have a lot to learn. Some of them get to a point where they realize they are no happier for all their efforts, and they become cynical and gloomy.

☿ Mercury

♑ Capricorn

10th House

Business Executive

Computer Whiz Kid is President of a successful company. On the whole, he enjoys the job in as far as it entails coming up with bright ideas and marketing strategies and delivering pep talks to the staff. He's not so happy with the pressure to get results because the Whiz Kid likes to do things for their own sake. Nor is he good at office politics. As long as he's firmly in control, he is okay, but if it looks like he's losing, he tends to panic.

With Mercury in Capricorn or Tenth, people are usually ambitious, needing to get ahead and keep moving to stay ahead. They are under a lot of pressure to achieve, and they frequently do. They are inclined to judge themselves and others by what they have, and especially by what *power* they have.

They will drive themselves relentlessly, doing whatever has to be done to achieve success. Charles Dickens is a famous example. Apart from writing his novels, he edited a magazine and took part in amateur theatricals and exhausting public readings of his works. Mercuries in Capricorn or Tenth are often pushy, direct, and confronting. Some of them lose their sense of proportion in the service of their ambitions and drives for success which, at root, are often fueled by fear of poverty and falling back to a lowly status. Richard Nixon had Mercury in Capricorn, which perhaps says as much as need be said about this aspect of the position.

Computer Whiz Kid can be good as a Social Worker as far as knowing a lot about the plight of humanity, thinking up schemes to alleviate it, and ways of making the public aware of the problems. As always, though, he doesn't relate to anyone at the level of feelings. In this job, the Whiz Kid might spend the morning enthusiastically working on some scheme that will benefit thousands of people. Then, when he goes to lunch, someone asks him for the price of a cup of coffee and he brushes by without a glance.

People with Mercury in Aquarius or Eleventh are often much concerned with justice, though it may be more indignation at injustice. They are very good at going through the right motions of something and making it look real. They have a good sense of what people in general want, though not what you, in particular, want.

The cry of Mercury in Aquarius or Eleventh could well be, "I love humanity. It's people I can't stand!" For advocating causes, crusading and standing up for their own and others' rights, these people are great. On the other hand, there is no one more inhumane and selfish when they are on the rampage in the grip of some crusading course of action. It's not that they disagree with your point of view; you are not allowed to *have* a point of view! Their feelings are so blocked that these Mercuries are liable to kid themselves they are acting logically and reasonably when they are really being driven by emotion.

☿ **Mercury**

♓ **Pisces**

12th House

Castaway

Marooned on a desert island, Computer Whiz Kid is at a loss. There is nothing he can use his technical skill on. His computer and mobile phone are of no use communicating with the animals or catching fish. He has no means of occupying his active mind and he is bored stupid. If he has been lucky enough to have a crate of whisky wash up with him, he will hit it hard. Otherwise, he will fall into a severe depression.

People with Mercury in Pisces or Twelfth tend to be introspective, concerned a lot with their own inner states and feelings. The more practically oriented ones can spend hours mentally rehearsing what they will say or do, or going over some poor performance so as to get it right next time.

Mercuries in Pisces or Twelfth can hardly be said to think. Not that they are unintelligent, but their thinking gets too mixed up with feelings, intuitions, and psychic impressions to really deserve the name. They get overwhelmed by other people's values and feel themselves to be outsiders. They are often able to grasp intuitively the essence of something, but are unable to put it into words—or, maybe, they don't *want* to put it into words because that would mean facing some unpleasant truth.

Typically, these people have a considerable air of withdrawal. They can be funny and witty, sometimes endearing, but it is a kind of substitute for intimacy. There is also a variety of Mercury in Pisces or Twelfth that is very taciturn and morose, speaking about three words a day.

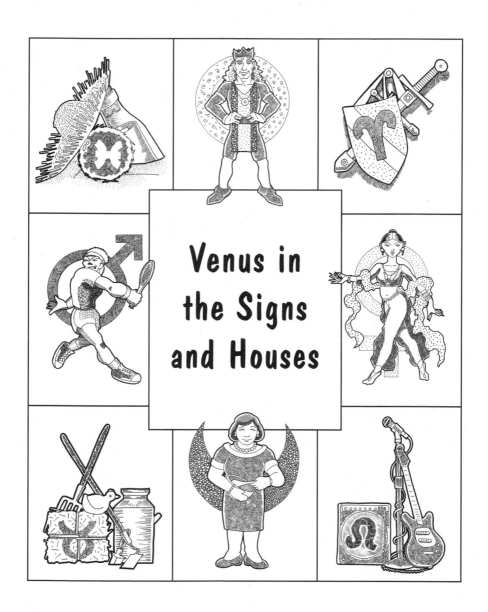

Venus in
the Signs
and Houses

Venus ♀

Aries ♈

1st House

Knight Errant

Being a Knight Errant is absolutely wrong for the Temple Dancer. For a start, she is encased in an ugly suit of armor and can't use her natural assets. She doesn't understand the idea of the Code of Honor because everything is intensely personal to her. The job brings out all her deep-jungle female survival instincts. She becomes a guerrilla fighter, seeing no shame in running away or attacking from ambush.

Venus in Aries or First people tend to be aggressive in relationships. They see everything in terms of conquest and are generally insensitive to what their partners might want. They often have considerable charm and magnetism, which comes from sexuality that is forced into a kind of over-drive and into areas of action that are not appropriate for it.

Venuses in Aries or First are full of exciting plans and can be stimulating company if you don't mind doing what *they* want all the time. They are the sort of people who will invite you for lunch at an expensive restaurant and order your meal for you before you arrive. If you like that kind of thing, okay, but the Venus in Aries or First person often comes to grief in relationships through sheer inflexibility and lack of communication.

♀ Venus

♉ Taurus

2nd House

Health Farm Manager

For the Temple Dancer, let's change being a Farmer to being the Manager of a health, beauty, and yoga farm. She does this job superbly. She makes the guests feel instantly welcome and inspires them with her own joy of living. The Temple Dancer lays a lot of emphasis on the importance of sexual fulfillment and makes sure there are always plenty of attractive men for herself.

People with Venus in Taurus or Second need a lot of stability in their relationships. They like to touch a lot and may literally be good at massage and similar healing arts. Rituals and routines make them feel good, and they are usually possessive to some extent. They are reliable and responsible, and are often turned on by the idea of solid, old-fashioned love and marriage that lasts a lifetime.

One way or another, sex is a big issue with the Venus in Taurus or Second person. They will be very concerned about getting it right and, if they can't, may give it up altogether and be totally celibate. Their possessiveness causes them problems in this way because they are reluctant to lose control. These people typically have a solid and sensible demeanor, though they are not always as practical and capable as one might expect. Partly this is because they like to have everything explained and to have a formula to deal with anything that turns up, but there are many situations that can't be handled by formulas and rituals. When the Venus in Taurus or Second person has to improvise and depart from a known routine, they are apt to come unglued.

Being a News Reporter splits the Temple Dancer in two, or rather, represses an important side of her. The aspect of the Temple Dancer that is an ordinary, lively young woman does the job well, mixing with people and being interested in them, using her charm, getting into situations where she can feel admired and, generally, satisfying her considerable curiosity. The more profound and cosmic part of herself has to be put aside. She sometimes feels that, though her life is interesting, it is a little thin in quality.

People with Venus in Gemini or Third have a great desire for experience and activity. Having a lot of friends and access to all kinds of information and gossip are ends in themselves for them. The idea of a puppy, happily exploring and maybe chewing up valuable objects, is not far from the idea of Venus in Gemini or Third. They are often great talkers and almost always interesting. They can be very sexy and flirtatious, but it's as well to be cautious with a Venus in Gemini or Third who is acting adoring and passionate. He or she may be less interested in you than in living up to some internal image of being a great communicator and good mixer.

Usually, they are fun to be with, but in rare cases they can be psychic vampires. You can spend an hour talking to this type and feel totally drained for no obvious reason. The conversation may have been lively, but the Venus in Gemini or Third was busy loading up on an interesting experience from you and not giving anything back.

♀ Venus

♋ Cancer

4th House

Baby Sitter

Temple Dancer finds herself rather confused about being a Baby Sitter. She like babies and likes taking care of them. Playing with the baby and doing all the little chores for her give her a lot of satisfaction. On the other hand, the job is very restricting. Temple Dancer has no outlet for her social and sexual energies. After a while, she starts to feel unappreciated. She becomes frustrated and moody, and possessive toward the baby.

People with Venus in Cancer or Fourth are inclined to feel that they are giving a lot, but that nobody takes much notice of them. Even when, in reality, they are getting a lot of attention, it doesn't seem to reach in and nurture them where they need it. This makes them disposed to do things to get themselves noticed even more, which may include a lot of moods and emotional game-playing.

These people can combine a crusty aggressiveness with a mute appeal for help. They go around with a kind of psychological "limp" that you are supposed to notice, but not *overtly*. The "limp" may be almost anything. Drinking too much or looking a little lost and undernourished are fairly common manifestations. People with Venus in Cancer or Fourth won't usually complain directly if they feel neglected; they are much too insecure for that. They are experts, however, in creating a big emotional issue out of some quite irrelevant situation and working off their feelings on that. They typically have a strong sexual nature, but it is kept in reserve in some way or there is something that has to be hidden and secretive about it.

Venus ♀

Leo ♌

5th House

Pop Star

Temple Dancer is great as a Pop Star. She throws herself into it, putting the songs across in a vigorous and sexy way. She knows exactly how to judge the mood of the audience and can be seductive, humorous, even self-mocking, according to what she senses will get them going the most. She always has to do encores and take a dozen curtain calls. The problem is that she enjoys herself so much that she gets locked into her public image and loses her gifts for intimate relationships.

All planets in Leo or Fifth need applause, but perhaps people with Venus there need it most. The satisfactions of love and sex often elude these people because there are so many other demands on their energy. Applause, limelight, and recognition of their frequently considerable talents become love substitutes.

Venus in Leo or Fifth people usually rely a great deal on their sense of humor and are often good at telling jokes and stories. Venus in the Fifth seems to me particularly a case where the house position is more significant than the sign. The Venus in Fifth person is more obviously "on stage," rather like Moon in Leo, but subtler. They are more serious and not as playful as the Venus in Leo type usually is; but all Venus in Leo or Fifth people have a regal quality, whether it is playfully extraverted or more dignified and reserved.

♀ Venus

♍ Virgo

6th House

Doctor

As a strictly professional and clinical Doctor, the Temple Dancer is at a disadvantage. Much as she might like to get it on with some of her more attractive male patients, she is not allowed to, so she becomes ultra-brisk and professional, concentrating on her work to the exclusion of her feelings. She feels constantly in danger of making a wrong move and wears a mask of caution and reserve.

People with Venus in Virgo or Sixth can be earthy, but rarely passionate. They often give the impression of having some overwhelming interest to which all relationships and emotional involvements have to take second place. This interest might be anything from collecting stamps to spreading spiritual enlightenment. In fact, they feel they have to be useful in order to be entitled to any love or affection. Like all people with planets in Virgo or Sixth, they never quite feel sure they come up to standard.

Venuses in Virgo or Sixth often retain a certain adolescent quality about their emotional lives. Love is apt to be an idealistic dream for them and they can get very critical and fussy about the reality. They are also inclined to see love and sex as needs they should satisfy in order to be well-rounded and healthy. On the whole, though, they would rather be working.

As a Party Hostess, Temple Dancer can express most of her true nature. She can go all-out to make herself as attractive as possible and be as sociable and flirtatious as she likes. She can't get too serious or involved with any one person, though, if she is to keep everybody happy. She has the knack for making each person feel as if they alone were the one she wants to be with. This is the secret of her success.

People with Venus in Libra or Seventh usually have a great deal of easy charm, which they can turn on or off as it suits them. They prefer to keep everything light and pleasant. Relationships are extremely important to these people, yet they often seem more than half afraid of them. Partly this is because they need to feel attractive and at peace with themselves. The emotional changes and disturbances that a serious relationship can provoke can endanger that, so they are everlastingly trying to maintain a state of balance between involvement and detachment.

Any kind of ugliness upsets them seriously and they hate to lose their cool. Their role model is Cary Grant—not that he had Venus in Libra, but he did create a strong Libra aura. He was charming, witty, and sophisticated, and this is what all Venuses in Libra or Seventh would like to be. Whether they achieve it or not is another matter.

♀ **Venus**

♏ **Scorpio**

8th House

Private Eye

Temple Dancer hates being a Private Eye. It is her nature to be open and trustful, but such qualities won't do her much good in this job. She becomes very neurotic, drinking and smoking too much and getting into the habit of joyless sex as a release from tension. Her self-respect takes a rather bad beating and she constantly wishes she could get into some other line of work or find some man who will take her away from it.

People with Venus in Scorpio or Eighth are apt to feel lonely, vulnerable, and misunderstood. Not that they will admit as much, except under extreme pressure. They like to keep themselves under tight wraps, though they are not necessarily all strong, silent types with an air of mystery and reserve. Some of them are. It depends on what else is in the chart. There are some Venuses in Scorpio or Eighth who let it all hang out and tell you all their little secrets—or so it seems, until you realize that you still have no idea what your Venus in Scorpio or Eighth friend actually *feels* about anything.

In relationships, they are either detached to the freezing point or extremely intense. They like to know *your* secrets and they don't feel entirely good about the relationship unless they are aware of one or two of your weaknesses. They have to have control, yet at the same time, they are always looking for someone who will control them.

Temple Dancer as a Political Foreign Correspondent—this is not that much different from being a domestic Reporter, except that the serious and profound side of her gets used more. She doesn't just cover the factual aspects of the story, but tries to find out what it means in a larger perspective. This tends to get her into more intimate involvement with her stories and contacts, but she has to see everything in terms of the job. Though she gets to know a lot of people very well, they are valuable to her more as contacts than as friends.

People with Venus in Sagittarius or Ninth like to have lots of adventures and relationships, amatory and otherwise. At least they like the *idea* of it, even if they go no further than a Walter Mitty fantasy. Though the person may be a staid, respectable stay-at-home, there will often be a boisterous and feisty quality somewhere. They are not afraid to be unconventional, nor to say what they think. Tactful they are not. In their eager pursuit of what they see as the truth, they can be completely insensitive to anyone else's feelings.

Often, they have a broad grasp of affairs and a certain ruthlessness. Both Winston Churchill and Margaret Thatcher have Venus in Sagittarius. Both were famous and, in some quarters, notorious, for their relentless sticking to harsh policies. A catch phrase associated with Mrs. Thatcher was, "There is simply *no* alternative!" You are likely to get that in some form from your Venus in Sagittarius or Ninth friend if you don't jump to it.

♀ **Venus**

♑ **Capricorn**

10th House

Business Executive

As Chairwoman of the Board, Temple Dancer is not much better off than the Housekeeper. She, too, becomes a shell of her real self, having to function in a world where power is everything and love is a weakness. Temple Dancer has more room for maneuvering than the Housekeeper. She is less inhibited about using her sexuality to make sure a deal goes through or to undermine the opposition. She is well aware that this is a horrible, perverted misuse of her energies, but she is stuck with the job and she has to do it the best she can.

People with Venus in Capricorn or Tenth can be earthy and passionate, but they usually have some kind of angle as well. They will rarely, if ever, make any kind of commitment before you do. The trouble is that you can never be sure that any commitment you make won't be used against you. Since people with Venus in Capricorn or Tenth will do that to you, they are always afraid of it being done to them.

Mercenary is perhaps too harsh a word to apply to *everyone* with Venus in Capricorn or Tenth. Maybe shrewd is closer to the mark. They will all want their payoff in some kind of social, financial, or career advantage. And, just as only a potential con-artist can be conned, so it often works out that these people end up being exploited themselves.

The Temple Dancer doesn't enjoy being a Social Worker for the same reasons the Housekeeper doesn't. She gets too bogged down in all the paperwork and the regulations. She feels sorry for the people she has to deal with and depressed by their often squalid lives. She thinks her efforts are probably not helping them much and doubts if they really can be helped. The Temple Dancer gets nothing of what she herself needs from the job and builds up a defensive personality of over-active concern, shutting out the troublesome questions.

People with Venus in Aquarius or Eleventh more often than not have a lot of social skill and ease. They can get along with just about anybody when in the mood, or they can be unwelcoming or morose when not. Their strangeness makes them intriguing and attractive. Lord Byron had Venus in Aquarius and he was pretty weird. He is a rather extreme example, but your typical Venus in Aquarius or Eleventh has something a little offbeat about them. This can attract some people, but the attraction is deceptive because these Venuses are basically cold and need to keep you at a distance. Getting close to a Venus in Aquarius or Eleventh can be like hugging a cuddly teddy bear and finding it is really a metal robot!

They do try, though. Most of them are good-natured and helpful, and will be kind to beetles and stray cats. They just aren't switched on in the passion department, though a special jolt can sometimes do the trick.

♀ Venus

♓ Pisces

12th House

Castaway

Being a Desert Island Castaway is a big treat for the Temple Dancer because it brings out the more cosmic qualities she hasn't been able to use so much in the other jobs. She is overwhelmed by the beauty of the island, the immensity of the sea and sky. She feels completely at home there and spends hours lying naked on the beach or swimming in the ocean, blissed out of her mind. This is what life is *really* about, she thinks. She feels sad, too, at the thought of all the other people who are missing it.

People with Venus in Pisces or Twelfth are usually sensitive and compassionate and want to do something for suffering humanity. Charles Dickens had Venus in Pisces and a lot of his writing was about exposing and removing the bad conditions under which so many had to live.

They can also be extremely self-indulgent and, though they may seem wishy-washy, they have a will of iron if they think their pleasures are being taken away from them. As with other planets in Pisces, these people don't quite live in the same world as the rest of the human race. Almost everyone with Venus in Pisces or Twelfth is dramatic and theatrical in some way. It's a different theatricality from Moon in Leo or Fifth, much more varied. These people tend to be dramatic about big cosmic and social issues where Moon in Leo or Fifth is just out for a good time. Of course, it is quite possible for the same person to have both combinations, in which case, they will be ultra-dramatic.

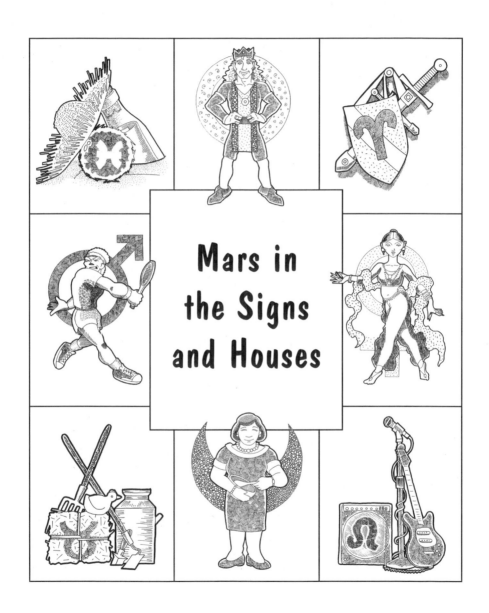

Mars in the Signs and Houses

It is sheer delight for the Tennis Champion to be a Knight Errant, better than playing tennis, because the rules are simpler. Nothing suits him more than to aim himself, his horse, and his lance at an opponent and go into an all-out, maniacal charge. He doesn't mind wounds. He'll go on fighting with blood streaming from a dozen cuts, still yelling, taunting, and issuing challenges. He gets the reputation of being the strongest and most dangerous knight. He eats dragons for breakfast, but doesn't know what to say to the damsel!

People with Mars in Aries or First usually have strong, clear, often simplistic views. They always want to *do* something about any problem. This is the kind of person who will keep any discussion firmly to the point, then stand up decisively and say, "Let's do it!" These people see life in terms of challenge and competition. All they think about is winning, and they have no patience with scaredy cats and losers.

In fact, they don't have much patience with anything. Waiting in line, or for a bus or train, is torture for the Mars in Aries or First person. It makes them savage and irritable, even those who are generally good-natured. These people are often generous and helpful if you ask them to do something. Just don't expect sympathy or concern for your feelings as well!

♂ Mars

♉ Taurus

2nd House

Farmer

Tennis Champion doesn't like being a Farmer. There is not enough scope for his initiative and aggression. If he has to do the job, though, he will do it vigorously. He spends his day rushing all over the farm, overseeing everything, yelling at the farm hands, rolling his sleeves up, and pitching in himself—sometimes when he would do better to leave the job to the expert. He exhausts himself trying to force things that can't be forced. He is half-convinced that there must be a way to harvest crops two days after sowing them, if only he could find it.

People with Mars in Taurus or Second will often have an air of contained energy, like a bee trapped in a glass jar. Sometimes they are outwardly slow, languorous, and slinky. Either way, they will focus a lot of their efforts on material gain and material pleasures.

Generally, they are very strong-willed once they have settled on a course of action; their enemies may call them stubborn and conservative. John F. Kennedy and Adolf Hitler both had Mars in Taurus. Both were capable of the same unrelenting pursuit of a goal, regardless of whether the people around them agreed with it or not. Much depends on how exhausted the Tennis Champion gets. Some people with Mars in Taurus or Second never get anything done because they are too bovinely content with things as they are.

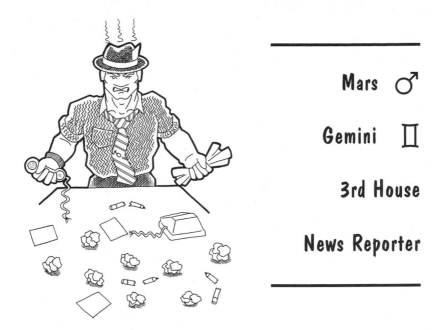

Mars ♂

Gemini ♊

3rd House

News Reporter

Being a News Reporter is not at all a bad job for the Tennis Champion. He likes the constant activity, the challenge of going for a story, and the sense of making things happen. What he doesn't like is having to deal with so many things at once or having stories come to nothing or getting taken off them. At the end of the day, TC often feels as though he's worked like a maniac, but doesn't have much sense of personal accomplishment to show for it.

People with Mars in Gemini or Third usually have a busy and bustling air about them, even if they are not actually doing anything. They are quite apt to change their line of thought in mid-sentence and go on to something else. They love to talk and they don't mind whether what they are saying is consistent or even sensible. Digression is an art form for them.

Their big problem is thinking that if they know something in their heads, they know all about it. They are not much on checking things by experience before coming to an opinion or a decision. Ideas, especially new ones, and conversations, especially stimulating ones, are like drugs to these people. A new idea can physically galvanize Mars in Gemini or Third out of a bad attack of boredom or lethargy. Boredom sets in quickly with these people. Rather than get to the depths of whatever they are doing, they will prefer to go off in pursuit of some new experience.

♂ Mars

♋ Cancer

4th House

Baby Sitter

The Tennis Champion is rather better at baby-sitting than we might have expected. After all, he is energetic and competent. As far as doing the things that need to be done, feeding and burping the baby, changing its diapers, and so on, he manages very well. What he is not good at is the feeling part of the job. He feels silly going "Oochy-koochy-koo!" and trying to soothe the baby when it cries. He finds himself uncomfortably aware of a whole world of feelings and vulnerability outside his scope, and he is relieved when the baby's mother returns.

There is a certain edgy defensiveness about people with Mars in Cancer or Fourth. They are generally quite assertive and outgoing, but you are always aware of boundaries with them. You can be having a free-ranging conversation with a Mars in Cancer or Fourth person until you unwittingly make some casual remark that sets off one of their defenses. Then there is an awkward silence or some reaction from them completely out of left field.

Almost always, Mars in Cancer or Fourth people are kind and considerate, and they place a lot of value on kindness. They will offer you anything out of their fridge and, quite possibly, forget the offer two minutes later if you have inadvertently made them crazy by touching on a forbidden area. They need to feel taken care of, but don't like to admit it, as that doesn't fit their image of being the strong ones doing the caring.

Mars ♂

Leo ♌

5th House

Pop Star

In the movie *Lust for Glory*, about General Patton, there is a scene where Patton has to apologize publicly for slapping a soldier. The actor, George C. Scott, gets up on the rostrum and says, "I thought I'd just stand up here and let you all see if I'm as big a son-of-a-bitch as you think I am!" This perfectly catches the flavor of Tennis Champion as Pop Star. He doesn't give a damn about pleasing the audience or getting them to love him. He's more likely to make a speech or give them a rousing pep talk than sing a song.

Mars in Leo or Fifth people are liable to say what's on their minds, and to hell with whether anybody wants to hear it or not. Frank Sinatra has Mars in Leo and he is famous for doing things "My Way." It's not that these people don't want recognition or applause. They do, as anyone with planets in Leo does—but they won't compromise to get it. If others don't admire them the way they are, too bad!

More often than not, people with Mars in Leo or Fifth have some creative talent. Even if they don't, they have abundant vitality and sexuality. Almost always, too, they are extremely, even extravagantly, generous. Think of Sinatra again. There is no doubt that these people are rather special, but they don't expect to have to prove it and they get mad if you don't recognize it. Of course, there is only a short step from this attitude to being pushy, arrogant, and dominating, which is what many Mars in Leo or Fifth people are.

♂ Mars

♍ Virgo

6th House

Doctor

As a Doctor, the Tennis Champion is, as always, energetic and competent. He is bluff and brisk and tolerates no nonsense from his patients, which often means that he ignores symptoms that are more emotional than physical. Because of this, his success rate of curing people is not as high as he would like. He gets dissatisfied with what he is doing and is forever trying new drugs and treatments that don't seem to work any better than the old ones. He can't understand why his colleagues, who don't appear to try so hard, are better doctors. He becomes critical and complaining, and blames his patients for not wanting to get well.

People with Mars in Virgo or Sixth are often chronically unable *ever* to be pleased or satisfied with *anything*. This can make them a pain to others and a misery to themselves. They always have to focus on what is wrong. I remember a small dinner party where everyone was having a marvelous time, laughing and enjoying themselves. Then a person with Mars in Virgo suddenly started talking about the possibility of nuclear catastrophe. He seemed to think it was a necessary corrective to the high spirits!

Being so conscious of things that are wrong, these people do make big efforts to put them right. Such efforts can range from worrying about doing the laundry to trying to change people's thinking on a big scale. Some notable gurus have had Mars in Virgo. At its best, the Mars in Virgo or Sixth type can be genuinely motivated by ideals of service to others and can make a big contribution. If only they could relax a little, though! These people don't know the meaning of the word "easy-going."

Being Maitre d' of a fashionable restaurant is the worst job of all for the Tennis Champion. A dozen times a day, he wants to punch a customer out or yell, "You cannot be serious, man!" when someone complains about the food, but he can't, not if he wants to keep his job. He spends his day with a phony smile on his face, being obsequious and charming, always doing what other people want and never what he wants. At the end of the day, his stomach is churning and his eyes bulging from his rising blood pressure. He heads straight for the nearest bar to help him calm down.

People with Mars in Libra or Seventh are often very successful, if only because they have learned how to charm and influence the right people. Yet they pay a high price for their success; there is always some feeling of extreme frustration or even victimization. Winston Churchill and Richard Burton both had Mars in Libra. Churchill spent most of his life in the political wilderness and suffered from what he called "black dog" depressions (as though there were a big black dog on his shoulders, complete with the mythic aura of evil). Burton openly complained of feeling victimized and, in many ways, wasted his talent on shoddy material.

There is a kind of chronic self-frustration going on all the time with the Mars in Libra or Seventh person. They usually have considerable charm and social skill, but it is on a rather superficial level. It fluctuates a lot, depending on how well they can suppress the angry turmoil going on within them.

♂ Mars

♏ Scorpio

8th House

Private Eye

As a Private Eye, the Tennis Champion can be as relentless and determined to win as he likes. He enjoys tracking down criminals, unearthing people's secrets, getting into big fights and confrontations. He has to learn to develop a poker face and devious ways, but that doesn't come too hard to him. Results are all that count, in his book, and the ends will always justify the means. He has to be sure he is in the right, though, and can't afford any doubts about his own abilities or the value of what he is doing.

People with Mars in Scorpio or Eighth often have this kind of confident, assertive demeanor. Some of them go about wearing an invisible sign saying, "I'm the best!" They are either very strong on integrity, insisting on doing the right and honorable thing all the time, or they are into all kinds of faking and skullduggery. The same person can exhibit both qualities. The secretiveness of Scorpio extends to themselves and they are adept at not letting their left hand know what their right is doing. A Mars in Scorpio or Eighth person is quite capable of complaining passionately about political corruption while filing a highly imaginative tax return. Whatever they are doing, they get fanatically involved with it. Some people call them obsessive, but they think of it as commitment.

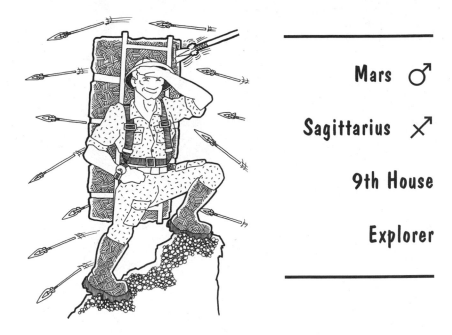

Mars ♂

Sagittarius ♐

9th House

Explorer

In some ways, the Tennis Champion is good as an Explorer. He enjoys the challenge and adventure, and being keyed up to meet the dangers of the new country. The problem is that TC is definitely not a team player, and that is what the job demands. He over-reacts to dangers or gets carried away by his personal pride and need for glory. He gets his party into battles with the natives that could easily have been avoided with a little tact. His hero is General Custer!

People with Mars in Sagittarius or Ninth typically have very strong views on how things should be done, and they express these views vigorously. Dustin Hoffman, noted as a perfectionist, has Mars in Sagittarius. D. H. Lawrence had Mars in the Ninth House. These people can't resist a challenge. If you know what pushes their buttons, they can be relied on to respond to the provocation and come out fighting every time.

Their great asset is that they are always open to bigger and better things. They are not strong on personal responsibility and would rather jump on a jet plane than deal with the problems of intimate relationships. You will find a fair number of workaholics with Mars in Sagittarius or Ninth. They can kid themselves that they are too busy with the job to deal with any mess they may have created in a relationship. I don't know if Richard Lovelace, who wrote the poem ending, "I could not love thee, dear, so much/Loved I not honour more" had Mars in Sagittarius or Ninth, but he had the right idea for it.

♂ Mars

♑ Capricorn

10th House

Business Executive

Chairman of the Board is quite a good job for the Tennis Champion. True, he has to curb his individuality to a large extent, but there is plenty of scope for his energy, aggression, and desire to win. His ability to focus on results and not worry about who gets knocked down in the process is very useful. He is good at setting goals and motivating his staff—mostly through fear and greed. The shareholders love him because he can be relied on to increase profits and create a wide sphere of influence for the company.

People with Mars in Capricorn or Tenth are usually energetic and ambitious. They can set long-term goals and pursue them untiringly. This can be the sort of person who, at the age of eighteen, has his career planned in detail right up to retirement. They prefer to work through conventional and accepted channels. For one thing, they are more likely to succeed if they are doing something everyone accepts.

Exceptions to this rule are more apparent than real. Aleister Crowley, who made a career out of being weird, had Mars in Capricorn. In his early life, he made a name for himself as a mountain climber and always had a longing to be accepted as a conventional English gentleman. When he embarked on his magical career, he took as his motto "Perdurabo," which means, "I will see it through to the end." That just about sums up the Mars in Capricorn or Tenth person. They never give up, never know when they are beaten. Every knock is a boost. (Sinatra has Mars in the Tenth.) This is often a highly admirable quality, but these people can be rather unsympathetic.

Mars ♂

Aquarius ≈

11th House

Social Worker

Tennis Champion hates being a Social Worker. Why should he waste his energy helping a bunch of layabouts who are too weak or lazy to do anything for themselves? He is contemptuous of his clients, but can get quite fanatical about broad schemes for eliminating poverty and improving public health. If he can get a job in planning or administration, he will be happy, but it makes his skin crawl to have to go into a low rent area and try to relate to the people there. He's glad to go back to the office and work on a plan for rehousing them in a new project.

People with Mars in Aquarius or Eleventh are often very rational, independent, and impatient with the way things are. New options and new ideas are food and drink to these people, and they will enthusiastically support any scheme for improving the world. Just don't come whining to them about your personal problems. Keep your messy, unscientific feelings well out of sight and you will get along fine with Mars in Aquarius or Eleventh.

They themselves are usually pretty well repressed, keeping their more passionate and earthy desires locked in a stainless steel vault, which means that they can be badly out of touch with themselves. They are apt to think that they are enlightened rebels when they merely have a chip on their shoulders, or that they are spiritually evolved when they are just fascinated by New Age ideas. Some of them really are enlightened rebels and spiritually evolved, like Carl Jung, who had Mars in the Eleventh House.

♂ **Mars**

♓ **Pisces**

12th House

Castaway

Marooned on a desert island, the Tennis Champion will either go to pieces entirely and lie in a cave all day, hopeless and depressed, or he will become a regular Robinson Crusoe, building a wooden house, cultivating a garden, and making weapons out of whatever comes to hand. It may be an uninhabited island, but TC can never be sure that a canoe full of cannibals won't show up any day. Whether he hides in a cave or builds a fort, the Tennis Champion is aware of feeling vulnerable and alone in a way he doesn't like.

People with Mars in Pisces or Twelfth can be weak and watery, or creepy, but more often they act tough. Two movie actors with Mars in Pisces illustrate the point. One is Vincent Price, who specialized in blood-curdling, creepy, and villainous roles. The other is Burt Reynolds, who laughs at himself playing the macho tough guy.

Perhaps more than most of us, the Mars in Pisces or Twelfth person learns to project and hide behind an image of some sort—Tough Guy, Good Scout, Sensible Girl, or whatever. They may act up front, but they will have a large reserve of secret desires and fantasies that you never get to see. Whether or not they act tough, they are usually gentle and compassionate, unless they feel threatened or frustrated. Then, they can act with incredible spite and ooze repressed anger all over the place.

Often, they literally prefer to work behind the scenes. I knew one Mars in Pisces man who ran a photographers' printing and developing service. This is a very concrete expression of the Mars in Pisces or Twelfth quality.

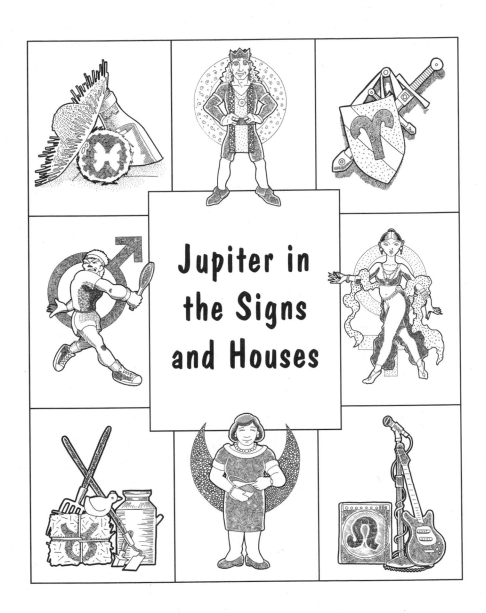

Jupiter in the Signs and Houses

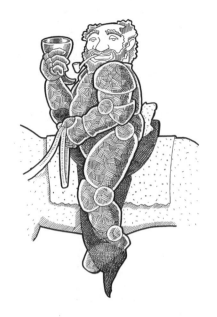

Jupiter ♃

Aries ♈

1st House

Knight Errant

As a Knight Errant, Favorite Uncle is an old campaigner. He knows how to make life easy for himself, always travels with a good supply of comforts, and doesn't do any more fighting than he has to. When he meets another Knight, he will be more likely to offer him a drink than combat. All the same, he is a firm believer in the institution of knighthood and its Code of Honor. It is just that, with age and experience, he has become wise in its ways and doesn't waste energy or go off on pointless quests. When he does fight, he fights honorably and gives a good account of himself, so the other knights admire and respect him.

People with Jupiter in Aries or First usually have an air of relaxed and expansive confidence. There can be a touch of world-weary pose in this. It's as if they go about wearing a T-shirt with the slogan, "No problem!" or "No biggie!" They seem to be equal to anything and will let you know it, rarely losing a chance to praise themselves. The boasting is very good-humored, and they are just as ready to tell a story to their discredit—in a humorous way that still makes them look good. Somehow, everyone else gets included in the boasting and self-praise, and a general air of good fellowship is created.

The archetypal Jupiter in Aries or First person is Falstaff—Shakespeare's fat knight. Falstaff was self-indulgent, always ready for good company, a meal, a joke, or a drink. As another character says of him, "My lord, he will drive you out of your revenge and turn all to a merriment." This is one of the great gifts of Jupiter in Aries or First.

♃ Jupiter

♉ Taurus

2nd House

Rancher

Favorite Uncle enjoys being a Farmer—in his case, it would be better to picture him as a big Rancher. He has the Midas touch. He goes on getting richer and more successful every year, and enjoys it all in an easygoing way as though wealth and luxury were just a normal part of living. As well, he loves being out in the open, working with the cattle, understanding nature and the rhythm of the seasons. This job makes him good-natured, tolerant, and well-liked by his workers and friends. He is a traditionalist and doesn't care for newfangled methods and ideas.

People with Jupiter in Taurus or Second have a strong sense of material values. It can manifest either as an earthy sensuality or a somewhat yuppie obsession with career and financial success. Either way, these people see their scope for improvement through being concerned with solid and tangible things. Often, they will focus strongly on physical health and appearance. Special diets, beauty aids, yoga, massage, and such have them drooling.

Their main problem is that they can overdo the contented placidity. Even when it is obviously in their own best interests to make a change of some kind, they frequently won't do it. There is a tremendous security need underlying all the material possessiveness and stubbornness. You rarely find a Jupiter in Taurus or Second person who isn't at least relatively well off, but they all have a fear of poverty deep inside.

Jupiter ♃

Gemini ♊

3rd House

Talk Show Host

For Favorite Uncle, let's change the Gemini job to being a Talk Show Host, which will bring out his nature better. He is good at the job and enjoys it, asking probing questions, being genial and welcoming, and getting people to talk about themselves, perhaps saying more than they had intended. But Favorite Uncle gets bored with the superficiality of the job. He wants to get deeper into what makes his guests tick than the format allows. Sometimes he gets very frustrated having to end an interview that was becoming interesting, and moving on to greet another guest.

People with Jupiter in Gemini or Third usually seem to be pursuing some elusive goal. If you ask them what it is, they can hardly tell you. Something drives them to be restless, inquiring, and dissatisfied. They have wide-ranging interests and can be on instant good terms with anyone. Two famous writers with Jupiter in Gemini were Charles Dickens and Lord Byron, both of whom not only wrote a lot, but produced extremely varied work.

What turns these people on most is novelty—opportunities to chase their will o'the wisp up ever new alleys. They throw themselves into each new project or relationship with great zest. The generosity of Jupiter comes out in the desire to teach and improve others. The others don't always want to be taught or improved, and your Jupiter in Gemini or Third can sometimes be a bit of a bore.

♃ Jupiter

♋ Cancer

4th House

Baby Sitter

Baby-sitting brings out all of Favorite Uncle's generous nature and big heart. He always shows up with lots of presents for the baby, and he has a large fund of bedtime stories, which he tells marvelously. Favorite Uncle knows how to talk to children and how to make them feel safe and looked after. He never talks down to them and is never authoritarian, always ready to play whatever game the child might want. The child's mother goes out knowing that her baby is in safe hands. Favorite Uncle does get rather conscious of the responsibility, though. The baby seems so fragile and vulnerable.

People with Jupiter in Cancer or Fourth usually have a strong urge to be generous and protective. They have big needs for security and comfort themselves, and they assume that other people do as well. They are at their happiest when they are "feeding" others in some way. Not necessarily with actual food, though Jupiter in Cancer or Fourth can be an excellent cook. The idea of "feeding" here includes giving presents, advice, and sympathy. These people often make good counselors because they are able to empathize with their clients.

The Jupiter in Cancer or Fourth person also has a very practical side—another reason they can be good cooks or counselors—and this can make them good at business too. Their main problem is that they overdo the protectiveness. A parent with Jupiter in Cancer or Fourth may well suffocate a child with excessive concern.

Jupiter ♃

Leo ♌

5th House

Pop Star

Favorite Uncle as a Pop Star is exactly like Frank Sinatra giving a concert. He is relaxed, confident, totally professional. He knows just how to appeal to his audience and has complete control from the moment he appears on stage to the moment he leaves. The secret is not so much that he sings well. It is more his own enjoyment of what he is doing, the pleasure of projecting his personality to so many people, his impeccable sense of timing. There's a level at which it's all showmanship. Under his relaxed good humor, he may be seething with anger about something in his personal or professional life.

Sinatra does, in fact, have Jupiter in the Fifth House. Along with their stablemates with Jupiter in Leo, these people seem to have endless resources of confidence and charm, which they can summon up at will, *provided* they get recognition and applause! I've seen it suggested that the reason Sinatra went on making public appearances for so long was that he needed the kick he got out of them. *All* Jupiter in Leo or Fifth people need this kind of boost from time to time, though not on such a big scale, admittedly.

They all need to be impressive, dignified, and yet playful, and to be treated as though they were glamorous and charismatic. If they don't get enough of this, their batteries run down and they can sulk as if they'd invented sulking. They are usually generous, not so much in the caring way that Jupiter in Cancer or Fourth is, but because it makes them feel good to make other people feel good. They can be overimpressed with their own performance and become arrogant, egotistical, and domineering. Vanity of one kind or another is always a danger for these people.

♃ Jupiter

♍ Virgo

6th House

Doctor

Favorite Uncle is in something of a quandary as a Doctor. He wants to help people and his generous nature is deeply touched by the suffering he sees. Yet he can't let himself get emotionally involved and he is aware that there are many ailments that neither he nor any other doctor can cure. This makes him extra conscientious. He keeps up with all the latest medical journals and is always looking for better and quicker ways to cure his patients. He has to learn to be philosophical and accept that, in the end, the cure lies with the patient, otherwise he will work himself into a breakdown.

People with Jupiter in Virgo or Sixth are almost always hard-working perfectionists, often with a particular idea or program they want to share with others. D. H. Lawrence, with Jupiter in Virgo, and his ideas about liberating sexuality, is one example. Werner Erhard, founder of the *est* training, with Jupiter in Sixth, is another.

This is another "workaholic" placement. These people never really let up on themselves; they are always seeking to provide service to others in one way or another. Because they are such perfectionists, this wears them down. They can become harried and rather humorless, in danger of needing so much service themselves that they can no longer give any. Generally, they are fantastically good organizers, with clear and tidy minds, though they are apt to get so immersed in detail they can't see the wood for the trees. But if you need a job done, and done well, the Jupiter in Virgo or Sixth person is the one to give it to.

Let's make Favorite Uncle an Ambassador for the Libra and Seventh job. He is excellent at it as he is fair-minded and genuinely concerned with finding solutions that are in everybody's interests. He has a large number of friends in the diplomatic, political, and business communities. Because of this, he is able to oil the wheels of diplomacy in informal, off-the-record meetings. He manages to please everybody, more or less, but, in being all things to all men, he sometimes feels he is losing his own identity.

Jupiter in Libra or Seventh people are, above all, concerned with being fair and reasonable. They are generally sincere in their relationships. Their need to treat everyone equally sometimes leads them to take completely opposed positions on some matter with different people. Then, if they don't sort the situation out quickly, they get accused of being two-faced. A lot of people with Jupiter in Libra or Seventh find it easier to be low profile because trying to accommodate everyone is very demanding. The danger then is that they become lazy, can't be bothered to take any initiative, and just passively allow things to go on as they are, however unsatisfactory that might be.

These people get out of touch with their own energy and find it hard to know what they want. This can make them so out of balance that they become insincere and opportunistic. They can get away with a lot, though, even at their worst.

♃ Jupiter

♏ Scorpio

8th House

Private Eye

Favorite Uncle is a Private Eye. Of course, he runs a big operation, with dozens of detectives working for him. He doesn't take on divorce or other sleazy business. He gets hired for jobs like investigating the backgrounds of political candidates and big cases of industrial espionage. His combination of experience, intuition, and ability to hire the best agents makes him unbeatable in his field. The need to keep so many secrets becomes a considerable burden, though, and goes against his open nature.

People with Jupiter in Scorpio or Eighth usually have a shrewd judgment of humanity and of situations, though they are also rather adept at convincing themselves that what they would like to be true *is* true. They need to protect their inner selves, and this leads to secrecy and reserve. That, in turn, often prevents them from using their judgment and resourcefulness as effectively as they might. Having power, especially secretly, is a big turn on for them.

They are often much concerned with getting to the roots of things and transforming them. We have Aleister Crowley, Werner Erhard, and Carl Jung as examples. Also on my list is a yoga teacher, a healer, and the man with Mars in Pisces who ran a photo lab. Working in the dark to transform blank film into pictures is a good, concrete manifestation of Jupiter in Scorpio or Eighth, especially when you add the fact that he had to be secret and confidential about what his clients were doing.

Jupiter ♃

Sagittarius ♐

9th House

Political Foreign Correspondent

Favorite Uncle is a Political Foreign Correspondent. This is the job he does best of all. With his wide range of contacts, his social graces, and acceptability, he has no trouble getting to know the things he wants to know. His vast experience and well-sharpened intuition enable him to see the way events are going long before anyone else. He can make a whole story out of a couple of lines of information and, more often than not, his speculations are right. He boosts his paper's circulation and gets a big salary in return. The problem is that people are apt to feel that they have been used by him, however graciously.

People with Jupiter in Sagittarius or Ninth are generally optimistic. They always just *know* they will win out. Sometimes they do! Their optimism and enthusiasm can be enough to work miracles for them. They tend to have their attention fixed on the big career goal and they can fall down on the practical steps needed to attain it. This may sometimes lead them to spend a hundred dollars to make a dime. They don't mind spending money, though, on themselves or other people. Generosity is their middle name, though their enemies might say "extravagance." They tip big and always have an ear and a kindly word for your troubles.

They can be a touch too impartial at times, too eager to move on to the next enlightening experience or big deal. Getting involved with a Jupiter in Sagittarius or Ninth person can be like having an exceptionally delicious Chinese meal. It's wonderful, but an hour later, you're hungry again!

♃ Jupiter

♑ Capricorn

10th House

Business Executive

As a hotshot Executive, Favorite Uncle is quite good, though at the expense of much of his real nature. The job forces him to be clinical and ruthless, and to do many things he doesn't like. If it is a choice between compassion and profits, then compassion will have to go. Still, he retains enough of his jovial, man-of-the-world quality to make an excellent leader, projecting his own self-confidence and optimism so that people trust him and are inspired by him. He always puts up a good front, which conceals the fact that he loses his nerve and judgment from time to time and makes some bad mistakes.

People with Jupiter in Capricorn or Tenth are great believers in discipline and hard work. The expression the Puritan Work Ethic was coined for these people. Mrs. Thatcher has Jupiter in Capricorn and she once said she didn't know the meaning of the word "leisure." Which is not to say that you won't find layabouts with this placing, but you won't find *happy* layabouts. They all feel they should be working twenty hours a day and achieving even if they aren't doing it.

These people love power and they don't always handle it well. Hitler also had Jupiter in Capricorn. One could certainly say he started out with idealism, but it quickly got very badly distorted. When these people feel threatened, they can be ruthless, and benevolence takes a back seat. They may feel sorry for you afterward, or even at the time, but if it is a question of You or Them, it will always be Them!

Favorite Uncle is distinctly ambivalent about being a Social Worker. His nature is to operate through personal generosity, but here he has to go by the rules. He feels sorry for the people he has to deal with, wants to help them in a more personal way, and feels guilty and frustrated because he can't. Since he can't do the job the way he wants, he has to work up enthusiasm, which he doesn't really feel, for the official plans and benefits. Like any convert who is a little doubtful of his faith, he will overdo his enthusiasm and protest too much.

People with Jupiter in Aquarius or Eleventh often have a rather naive faith in systems and ideas, especially if these have a humanitarian or "New Age" flavor. They are inclined to think that planning, talk, and propaganda are sufficient answers to everything, that others will see the *reason* in what they are saying and change their ways. Of course, it doesn't work like that, and people with Jupiter in Aquarius or Eleventh often seem to be shouting very loudly to convince themselves. D. H. Lawrence, with Jupiter in Eleventh, is a good example of this. At the time he was writing so enthusiastically about sex, he was actually impotent. This is a fate that, in one form or another, not necessarily sexual, seems frequently to overtake Jupiter in Aquarius or Eleventh. They are so reasonable, and they seem to imagine that talking about feelings is the same as feeling them. Consequently, they create an overdetached and uninvolved aura that makes it hard to relate to them on an emotional level.

♃ Jupiter

♓ Pisces

12th House

Castaway

Though we have seen Favorite Uncle as a highly social person up to now, he is also happy to be marooned on a desert island. Like Temple Dancer, he has a religious and cosmic side to him that can emerge in solitude. He doesn't do the Robinson Crusoe act. He makes the minimum arrangements for his survival and spends a lot of time in deep meditation, sending out good vibrations for the benefit of humanity, or perhaps writing a book of guidance and wisdom. Away from the hustle and bustle of everyday life, he comes to see how stupid and wasteful much of it is.

People with Jupiter in Pisces or Twelfth are usually attuned to the sufferings of humanity. They want to go out and feed the starving millions of the world, or, of course, they may be so disturbed by these sufferings that they shut them out of their minds altogether. In either case, these people are typically compassionate and thoughtful. They enjoy, in fact *need*, periods of solitude; they can go for weeks without much contact with others and not feel lonely because they have such rich inner resources to draw on. Naturally, this depends on how developed the person is and on other things in the chart.

Pisces is always a paradoxical sign, whatever planet is in it. Although people with Jupiter in Pisces or Twelfth are introspective, they are also reluctant to face the parts of themselves they don't like. They tend to have an image of themselves as good, caring people and they are adept at turning a blind eye to their less desirable qualities. They also get into trouble because they expect others to read their minds, and they rarely communicate clearly.

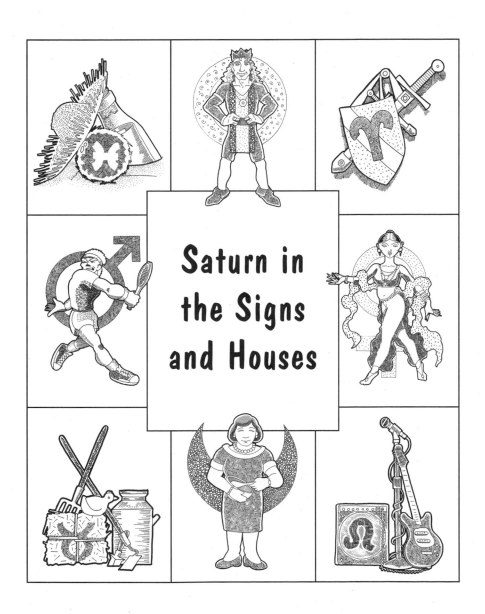

Saturn in the Signs and Houses

The Old Math Teacher is appalled by the entire business of being a Knight Errant. To him, it is just a lot of schoolboy nonsense with no logic or reason behind it. The first thing he does is get up a petition to have the whole thing stopped. It's too much of a personality cult, he claims. The knights should stop fighting each other and work as a team, doing something worthwhile. Of course, what's really bothering him is that he is too old and stiff in the joints for the job and is afraid of getting hurt!

People with Saturn in Aries or First are pretty much loners. They feel they haven't quite got the energy or nerve for a really active life. They can't get excited by anything that calls for them to shine in public or be first in any way, yet this is what they secretly want. They feel guilty about their own needs for excellence. If the Saturn in Aries or First person takes a stand on anything, or asks for what they really want, they are afraid people will say, "Who do you think *you* are?"

They feel they have to be mediocre in order to survive. Saturn in Aries or First is the kind of person who starts work at 8:00 A.M. and goes home at 5:00 P.M. every day of his or her life. They create a kind of emotional island of banal routine for themselves. As long as nothing invades it, they are happy—moderately so, of course.

♄ Saturn

♉ Taurus

2nd House

Farmer

In some ways, the Old Math Teacher does well as a Farmer. He is conservative, believes in using tried and tested ways of getting the most from his farm. He doesn't care to experiment with any innovations. He is patient, able to make long term plans and wait for the results. On the other hand, he expects everything to work out according to his calculations and he finds it hard to adjust to difficulties caused by the weather, predators, and disease, all of which he has no control over. He wants to run the farm as though he were working out an equation and gets very testy and irritable when he can't.

People with Saturn in Taurus or Second often seem to be motivated by a fear of poverty and loneliness, and they try to run their lives to a schedule to keep the fear at bay. This means that they usually have very definite and limited tastes and are hard to please. They are not rewarding people to give presents to. Sometimes, though not in all cases, they can be lazy and apathetic. They like to stick with things they know will work and don't care to make too much effort for themselves. This is often the result of depression, which these people are inclined to suffer from.

The person with Saturn in Taurus or Second sees survival in terms of comfort and physical security. They identify closely with their possessions and make a kind of defensive wall out of them. They hate any kind of surprises, even good ones, but they can be very generous and hospitable as long as you don't take them for granted. If you do, they get mad.

Saturn ♄
Gemini ♊
3rd House
News Reporter

As a News Reporter, the OMT despises what he has to do. He can't understand why people should be interested in the trivial and often sordid stories he has to deal with. As always, though, he will do the job thoroughly, despite his feelings about it. His biggest assets are his encyclopedic memory and his ability to organize the information he gets and see how it relates to other stories. In fact, he would be happier with a job as the paper's archivist or librarian. He would still think the material trivial, but at least he would be using his talents. As it is, he feels frustrated and nervous most of the time.

People with Saturn in Gemini or Third know a lot, or like to think they do. They pride themselves on being competent and well-informed, and this gives them a feeling of security. They can't bear to be proved wrong or thought ignorant about even the most trivial thing, and they will rarely admit a mistake. If they take a wrong turn when driving with you as a passenger, they will blame *you* for it!

Generally, Saturns in Gemini or Third are observant and have a capacity for learning quickly, but this is another planetary placing in which people mistake having information for thorough knowledge of a subject. They will offer advice on any matter under the sun, but if you tell them something they don't know or offer any kind of help, they are insulted. How dare you question their competence or intelligence! The unwillingness to learn anything other than what they have already decided they want to learn leads them to be very skeptical and cynical about any kind of new approach to old problems.

♄ Saturn

♋ Cancer

4th House

Baby Sitter

Baby-sitting is the worst job of all for the Old Math Teacher. He has no idea how to relate to children. They make him extremely nervous with their outspoken and, to him, irrational physical and emotional needs. He can never relax and enjoy being with the child. He is always afraid of something going wrong and spends his time thinking of excuses to cover himself in case the mother should be angry when she comes home. Only when the child is safely asleep does the OMT begin to feel slightly easy. Even then, he has to look in every ten minutes to make sure she is still breathing.

People with Saturn in Cancer or Fourth find it very difficult to develop any sense of emotional security. They spend a good deal of time in self-protective maneuvers of one kind or another. These can include becoming very rich and successful. We can instance Frank Sinatra again, with Saturn in Cancer. It is a substantial part of his magic that he conveys so well feelings of being lost, vulnerable, and deprived of love (like the baby with the OMT in charge!)

He also illustrates well that these people almost always have a tough, invulnerable public image, rather like the Mars in Pisces and Twelfth crowd. This, of course, completely wrecks any chance that someone might get close to them and heal their insecurities. There is a line in one of Raymond Chandler's novels where his private eye, Philip Marlowe, reflects that there is no cure for loneliness except the cold, empty heart that needs nothing from anyone. This is all too often the way people with Saturn in Cancer or Fourth will handle their fears.

As a Pop Star, the Old Math Teacher is a complete frost. He has a harsh, creaking voice and is quite incapable of letting go enough to put a song over. Indeed, he thinks doing such a thing would be childish showing off. But here he is at the microphone and he is expected to do something. Perhaps he will discuss a mathematical theorem. Whatever he does, the audience is going to be very bored. The OMT feels stupid and self-conscious, yet also feels an obligation not to let himself down by failing the test. How did he let himself get talked into this absurd situation?

People with Saturn in Leo or Fifth frequently have considerable creative talent, yet they feel uncertain about it, not sure they are good enough, and especially, feel that what they do is never quite *right* for the people concerned, however good it might be in itself. They have a lot of pride; they want to be recognized and applauded, yet they feel they don't deserve it and often go entirely the wrong way about getting applause and recognition.

Meanwhile, they cover up their uncertainty and need for love by being rather rigid and reserved, sometimes inclined to dominate or bully. This is not always straightforward. Some of them do it by whining, appearing weak and needy, yet playing manipulative games that somehow leave you on the wrong foot. This is another rather bad position for a parent/child relationship. The Saturn in Leo or Fifth person is too insecure about his or her own inner child to be able to give the right kind of attention to an actual child. In extreme cases, this can indicate child abuse.

♄ Saturn

♍ Virgo

6th House

Doctor

As a Doctor, the Old Math Teacher has some of the same problems he does as a Farmer. He knows his job backward and forward, and he can't understand why his patients don't always get well when he gives them the correct treatment. He gets even more upset with those patients who don't take his advice and then get well all the same, especially if they are cured by some form of alternative therapy. The fact that things don't always work by the book erodes the OMT's confidence. He spends a lot of time worrying and trying to improve his skills and knowledge. He feels his responsibility to his patients too keenly to be able to take the view that something has to be left to nature.

People with Saturn in Virgo or Sixth seem to feel that some big secret of life is always eluding them. They can be incredibly persistent, nagging, and analytical, apparently unable to see that there are some areas of life that can't be dealt with by reason or logic. They *act* as if they had the solution to everything. Like unmarried marriage counselors, they will confidently hand out advice on matters they have no personal experience of and know only in theory. In the next breath, they will put on a great show of humility and assure you that there are many things they don't know.

If your average Saturn in Virgo or Sixth person feels doubtful about their own efficiency and competence, they will boost their ego by pointing out how wrong and inefficient other people are. These people hate anything that is outside their familiar scope, and they will interpret friendly gestures as intrusions almost as readily as Saturn in Gemini or Third.

Saturn ♄

Libra ♎

7th House

Ambassador

The Old Math Teacher makes an excellent Ambassador. In a lot of ways, this is a job he can do as if he were working out an equation. He has a fine sense of formality and protocol, is always honorable in his dealings, and genuinely attempts to promote international harmony. He is not loved and popular in the way Favorite Uncle is because he is too reserved and austere, but he is widely respected. This, as well as his complete grasp of the political situation, is what makes him so good at the job. He can see things that are slightly off balance well before they get out of control, and he works to put them right.

People with Saturn in Libra or Seventh live a curious paradox. They can't really do without close relationships, yet they are terrified of commitment and involvement. One result of this is that they feel they have to work hard at their relationships. The women in particular are forever wondering what small nuances in their partner's behavior really mean and they are full of schemes and plans for keeping things on an even keel. The men are the same, but women are more open about it.

Mostly, these people are tactful and kind. They feel responsible for other people and never quite trust them to do things right. They have a complicated mental agenda for how they and everyone else should behave, and they are constantly on the watch for infringements of protocol. It is not easy to be spontaneous around your average Saturn in Libra or Seventh person.

♄ Saturn

♏ Scorpio

8th House

Private Eye

As a Private Eye, the OMT is very good at finding clues, making the right deductions, and catching the culprit. However, he can't stand dealing with the sleazy mess of human emotions, blood, and tears that also goes with the job. It makes him uncomfortable in the same way, only worse, that the child's needs did when he was baby-sitting. In this job, though, he can more easily keep the messiness of emotion at a distance. He adopts an attitude of cold professionalism, deploring emotion in his clients and denying it in himself. Sherlock Holmes is not a bad image of Saturn in Scorpio or Eighth.

People with Saturn in Scorpio or Eighth are good at being alone. They are reserved and controlled. They may *act* sexy, and perhaps it is not all an act, but they have very definite inner limits as to how much they are really prepared to trust and let go. Their secret ideal is the same as Saturn in Cancer or Fourth, the cold empty heart that needs nothing from anyone. However, Saturn in Scorpio or Eighth not only acts tougher than in Cancer or Fourth, it *is* tougher. The deep, inner torment is probably greater, nevertheless. These people can be destructive and jealous, far too skeptical for their own good, and cruel, both deliberately and unconsciously.

They are in a big dilemma. What they really need is to be able to confront and talk out their painful and vulnerable feelings, but their pride won't even allow them to admit such feelings exist, not to anyone else, anyway. They turn their energies outward and make a powerful impression on the world one way or another. You don't find many nonentities with Saturn in Scorpio or Eighth.

Saturn ♄
Sagittarius ♐
9th House
Explorer

The Old Math Teacher has become an Explorer, leading his party into unknown territory. He has to have some worthy motive for doing this in the first place, perhaps to bring the benefits of civilization to the natives. Consequently he feels burdened and responsible. The project seemed easy enough back at headquarters. Out here on the ground, he begins to think he has taken on more than he can handle. He is overcautious, stopping to take compass bearings and other checks and inventories far more often than is necessary. He slows the expedition down and gets on the nerves of the other members of the party.

People with Saturn in Sagittarius or Ninth seem to have strong and impregnable self-esteem, though those around them may not understand why they should have. They are usually extremely ethical and trustworthy, even if they also take themselves a little too seriously. They are ambitious and can be materialistic, taking on too much in their eagerness to achieve. They are apt to talk a lot about freedom and how much it means to them, but they will run a mile rather than accept real freedom. Their idea of freedom is to be rich and famous so that they can do what they like and enjoy the good things of life.

This is another group that is likely to have a longterm life plan, with their career goals mapped out almost as soon as they are out of the cradle. Their worst problem is that they can be very dogmatic and judgmental, unable to compromise on anything.

♄ Saturn

♑ Capricorn

10th House

Business Executive

The Old Math Teacher does very well as Chairman of the Board. It's a job that calls on his powers of reasoning and logic and ability to work for a result without getting involved in side issues. He plans thoroughly, makes sure he knows all he needs to know, and keeps firm control and supervision of all his projects—too much so, not allowing his subordinates enough initiative. If someone is not up to the job, the OMT will get rid of him with no more compunction than if he were correcting a mistake in a calculation. He is cautious about new projects and sometimes loses good business through his unwillingness to take an occasional risk.

People with Saturn in Capricorn or Tenth are above all concerned with ambition, career, and achieving concrete goals, and so making themselves accepted and respected. If they can't make it in terms of money and status, they feel worthless and undeserving. Generally, they have a deeply melancholy streak, and they can be hard and unfeeling. Don't tell your troubles to a Saturn in Capricorn or Tenth unless you are paying them for their time or are at least willing to *do* something about your troubles. These people hate to be dumped on. At the same time, they feel they *should* be responsible for you and feel guilty for not wanting to be.

It's probably true to say that something went wrong with the parenting of the Saturn in Capricorn or Tenth people. The result is that they fear they will never be adequately nourished or rewarded. They never are either, and that's the drive that keeps them going.

Saturn ♄

Aquarius ≈

11th House

Social Worker

The Old Math Teacher approaches being a Social Worker with the same attitude he had to being a hotshot Executive. We can best think of him as having transferred from running a successful company to heading up a big charitable organization. It is not much different for him except that he is no longer concerned with profits but with improving conditions and relieving misery for large numbers of people. In the nature of the thing, he can't exert as much control as he did in the other job. He has to be a little more open, and his subordinates will press some fairly weird and outrageous plans on him from time to time. He finds it difficult to assess these accurately, which causes him considerable problems.

People with Saturn in Aquarius or Eleventh are generally good organizers, either of people, in the case of Albert Schweitzer, or of concepts, as with Lord Byron and Carl Jung. They are perhaps not so good at organizing themselves, and a tendency to go along with wild and extreme ideas may get in the way of actual achievement. They tend to get locked into systems of ideas and values that are logical and consistent, but not very practical or realistic. This is true of the three people just mentioned and even more of Aleister Crowley, who also belongs here.

Saturn in Aquarius or Eleventh people all put a lot of value on social action, doing things in groups, being organized and scientific. Once they have adopted an idea, they can be very dogmatic and unyielding. These people are not big on empathy and compassion. They want to do you good, but if they have to break your legs to fit you into their system, so be it!

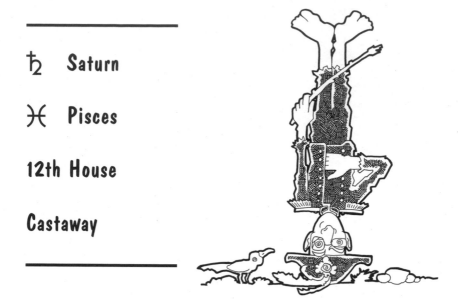

♄ Saturn

♓ Pisces

12th House

Castaway

The Old Math Teacher is utterly disoriented by being marooned on a desert island and he goes straight into a psychotic breakdown. The one thing he must have is structure, and here there is no structure of any kind. He functions by knowing and obeying the rules and, on the desert island, all is chaos, or so it seems to him. None of his knowledge is of the least use to him. The only way he can cope is to let go of all that he knows and learn to survive from scratch, which is almost impossible for him to do.

People with Saturn in Pisces or Twelfth are very sensitive and emotional. They are so open and vulnerable to the pressures of life that they usually develop a strong defense against this part of themselves and may seem very self-assured and tough. Under whatever hard surface they present, they worry a lot and are subject to all kinds of fears and imaginings, which they may know are not grounded in reality, but which plague them nevertheless.

Not all of their apprehensions are illusory, of course, and they are capable of deep intuitive compassion. It is not easy for them to use this, nor the psychic powers that they frequently have, because they are afraid of anything irrational. These are the kind of people who can deal with astrology only by dismissing it or trying to prove it with statistics. In their fear of the non-rational, more dark and feminine side of life, they will gladly distort their own natures and turn themselves into super-rationalists.

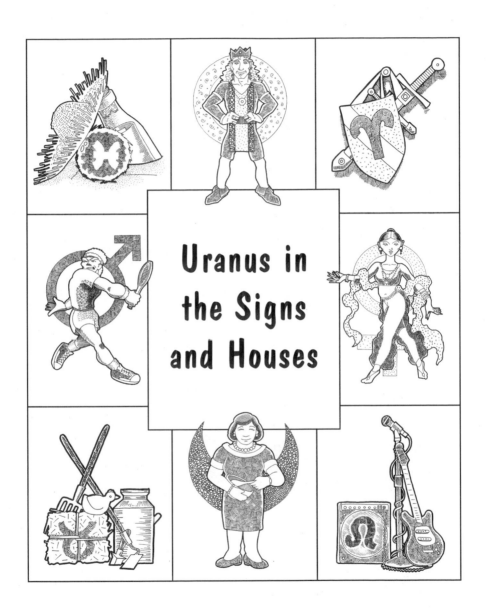

Uranus in the Signs and Houses

The Planets Beyond Saturn

The rule that house position has greater weight than sign position applies even more to the planets beyond Saturn. Uranus, Neptune, and Pluto stay in each sign for so long that they have only a general background effect on the person as far as the sign is concerned. We don't, for example, consider Uranus in Leo as adding to the Leo effect in the chart, but Uranus in the Fifth House will definitely be felt.

From now on, we will consider only the house placings. Each of these planets will overwhelm the job they have to do by their strange, other-dimensional energies.

Uranus ♅

1st House

Knight Errant

We can imagine Crazy Inventor, like Mark Twain's Yankee at the Court of King Arthur, as a Time Traveler transported to the days of chivalry and Knights Errant. He refuses to take any of it seriously. He invents a ray that magnetizes everyone's armor so that their weapons stick to them and they can't fight. Instead of killing the dragon, he shoots it with a tranquilizing dart, then tames it and takes it around on show. He introduces smoking to the court and turns out a nice line of dragon-shaped cigarette lighters.

People with Uranus in First invariably have something vivid and striking about them. The person may come on like a creep, but at least he will be a notable creep. More usually, there is a sense of tremendous energy and purpose, even though the person may not know what to do with it. These people have an intense, electric quality and will frequently say and do unconventional or downright outrageous things. Dickens, Byron, and Crowley had Uranus in First. They all behaved as if they didn't give a damn what anyone thought of them—especially Byron and Crowley, who both made a career of it!

Their problem is loneliness. They are generally so unusual in their behavior and so out of synch in their ideas that it is difficult for them to find anyone similar. Crowley used to begin every conversation by saying, "Do what thou wilt shall be the whole of the law." A Uranus in First woman I used to know introduced herself to me by bluntly telling me, as I was about to go on stage in an amateur performance, that my costume was wrong! This is fairly typical.

♅ Uranus

2nd House

Farmer

When the Tennis Champion was a Farmer, he got impatient because he couldn't harvest his crops two days after planting them. Crazy Inventor soon solves this problem. In fact, he's working on a time-distortion device that will enable him to harvest the crops before he plants them! The farm runs with tremendous efficiency—sometimes. We have to remember that our character is a *crazy* inventor, and some of his ideas don't work very well. He'll change horses in midstream just because he's been told not to, and spend the rest of the day sitting in the river figuring out a way to get across.

People with Uranus in Second have an unusual, not to say eccentric, attitude to material possessions. They can be broke one day, rich the next, then broke again because they invested everything in some hare-brained project, which sometimes makes them twice as rich! One Uranus in Second man I know gave up his marriage, big house, and thriving business to go live in another country with a woman he had known for only a few weeks. It worked out well, too.

These people can get into difficulties that would leave the rest of us breathless, and they usually manage to get out of them or turn them to advantage. They frequently make their money in unusual, even outrageous ways. Famous Uranus in Second people include Ron Hubbard, who invented a new religion, Scientology, to make money. There is also Alan Watts, who made money writing about Eastern religions long before they became fashionable, and Lewis Carroll, the mathematics professor who wrote *Alice in Wonderland*.

Uranus ♅

3rd House

News Reporter

Crazy Inventor as a News Reporter—he never keeps a job for long because his ideas about what makes a good story are too screwy. If he can't find anything nutty enough to appeal to his sense of humor, he'll make something up. The paper keeps him in reserve to write the April Fool's Day spoof, when he turns out a deadpan article about a proposal to decimalize time or a process for extracting gasoline from seaweed. He is always coming up with bright new schemes for improving the printing of the paper or gadgets that help the reporters get their stories in faster.

People with Uranus in Third communicate in some kind of eccentric way. They can't be bothered to observe the conventions that most of us use in conversation. Actually, you don't find many pure Uranus in Third types around. They usually learn to suppress it if they want to get along.

One who didn't was Lenny Bruce, the Sixties comedian who outraged his audiences with bad language and blunt discussion of taboo subjects. He wrote a book called *How to Talk Dirty and Influence People*. If it had been "weird" rather than "dirty," the title would have done for almost any Uranus in Third. Champion of the lot was Nicolaus Copernicus, the fifteenth-century astronomer who first showed that the earth goes around the sun, not the other way, as had always been thought. The way he communicated didn't just upset people's prejudices, it changed their entire conception of the universe. These two are extreme examples. The average Uranus in Third person will probably be no more than distinctly informal.

♅ Uranus

4th House

Baby Sitter

Pity the poor child who gets Crazy Inventor as a Baby Sitter. She won't be cuddled, fed, or put to bed on time. She will be kept up all night playing some computer game that Crazy Inventor has brought, or be expected to listen intelligently while he goes on about quarks, black holes, or chaos theory. It will be a memorable experience for her. She may well find the novelty exciting, then be tired for a week or off her food. Mother will be furious when she gets home and will write an angry letter to the baby-sitting agency.

People with Uranus in Fourth usually seem to have an iron will and implacable determination to do what they want. Mrs. Thatcher ("There is simply *no* alternative!") and Frank Sinatra ("I did it my way.") are good examples. They are not afraid to stand up and be counted and, if they are in a position to do so, to push through programs of radical reform against all opposition. (Mrs. Thatcher again, and also John F. Kennedy.)

There is a basic coldness about them; they will take note of your ideas, but your feelings don't affect them in the least. They often live in domestic circumstances that are strange in some way or not what they seem. The sense of identity and security of Uranus in Fourth people is constantly disrupted. More than most, they will consciously invent a consistent identity for themselves to compensate for the deep sense that they are walking a tightrope.

Crazy Inventor is quite happy, as a Pop Star, to get up in front of a microphone and make a fool out of himself; but the audience won't get what they expected. He'll probably sing some fast-moving patter song or walk on his hands while singing a song in Basque or Zulu. Whatever he does, it will draw attention to his cleverness rather than entertain the audience. Some of the audience might be pleased, but most of them will ask for their money back.

People with Uranus in Fifth usually strike you first as being proud. They might be proud and reserved, though more often they are attention-getting in some way. Often, they are very good looking and are conscious of the fact, especially the women. Since one of the meanings of Fifth House is love affairs, they will be very unconventional in this area. Don't expect a quiet life if you get involved in a love affair with one of these people. They are liable to see a stranger across a crowded room and fall instantly in love, only to be bored and disappointed with the person when they have fought their way through the crowd to him or her!

Children are also connected with the Fifth House, and people with Uranus here are not usually happy with the role of parent. The sooner the kid grows up and can be treated as an equal, the better. A good many Uranus in Fifth people will avoid having children altogether. It ties them down too much.

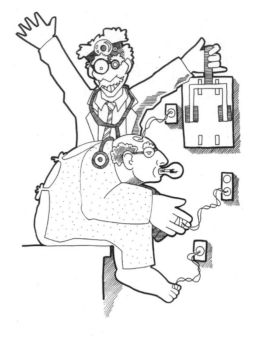

♅ Uranus

6th House

Doctor

Crazy Inventor has no patience with the restrictions of being a Doctor. He'll try anything he thinks might cure his patients, such as acupuncture, faith healing, or hypnotism. He'll even give them some pills now and then. If he doesn't get struck off the medical register—and if he does he'll set up as an alternative practitioner—he will rapidly acquire a list of oddball patients. Everyone that other doctors have given up on will come to him. Sometimes he really does perform miracle cures.

People with Uranus in Sixth don't settle down easily to steady employment. If they try to, they are liable to find their efforts disrupted by health problems. They are much happier to be doing something freelance, and happier still if what they are doing is out of the ordinary. In my list of people with Uranus in Sixth, there are two astrologers and a yoga teacher.

None of the people with Uranus in Sixth like to do routine stuff. They all hate to do housework. This position of Uranus often results in a very active life. A good many highly creative people, especially musicians, have it. You get entrepreneurs with Uranus in Sixth who have an interest in a dozen businesses, and artists who can express themselves in several media and who like to change their style radically every so often. On the other hand, you also find examples of people with Uranus in Sixth for whom all this disruptive energy is too much. They give up on it and cruise through life in a low-key way, but there will always be something disruptive about them or their circumstances.

Uranus ♅

7th House

Maitre d'

Crazy Inventor just about manages to keep his job as a Maitre d' by getting known as a character. He shows up to work in a T-shirt, jeans, and sneakers, amid the immaculately and formally dressed waiters. He insults his customers. Instead of saying, "Good evening, sir." he will say, "What the hell are you doing here again?" or, "Everything's off!" When the mood is on him, he'll invite a street crazy in, give him the best table, and seat his most influential customers in a dark corner near the kitchen or the restroom. Since the restaurant genuinely is good, apart from him, the customers convince themselves they enjoy his antics.

People with Uranus in Seventh don't really know how to behave in relationships. They often seem to have the peculiar idea that others will love them for their independent, awkward, and original attitudes—which doesn't work, of course. They may be admired, or respected, but never loved. They get people mad, and make them jealous and competitive. People they thought were friends—to the extent that anyone with Uranus in Seventh *has* any friends—turn against them in unexpected and unpleasant ways. Or the Uranus in Seventh person does the turning. If you don't buy their act, you are liable to find they have shut you out of their lives. No hard feelings—just a cold, clinical "zap!"

There is an integrity about Uranus, and you can generally trust these people to honor their commitments; but you can't trust them for any depth or constancy of feeling.

♅ Uranus

8th House

Private Eye

Crazy Inventor as a Private Eye is in a similar position to when he was a Doctor. He'll use *anything* to solve the problem and catch the criminal. He'll have a battery of computers and scientific techniques, but he'll also use astrology, tarot, magic, or psychic powers if these serve his purpose. He's not much interested in the morality of the job, and the sleaze doesn't bother him. He wants to get to the bottom of things to increase his own power and influence. He's quite capable of switching sides, just for the experience, and being a criminal for a while.

People with Uranus in Eighth are generally passionate and intense. They are not usually very sympathetic because they are too driven by their own demons to relate very well to anyone else. The passion may be deeply hidden, and they may well present a distinctly cool and invulnerable front to the world. This is because they are afraid of being burned up entirely by their inner fires if they give way to them.

They are highly possessive, though again, they may not let it show. If you cross one of these people, you will not lightly be forgiven. All may seem well on the surface, but ten years later, if you are in a difficult position, your Uranus in Eighth friend may not be able to resist putting the boot in. This means, of course, great will power and persistence, to hold a grudge so long, which these people can also put to better use.

Uranus ♅

9th House

Explorer

Crazy Inventor leading an exploration through the unknown jungle is either a big inspiration to his party or an equally big liability. They will never know which it is from one day to the next. He will be struck with brilliant ideas and intuitions at the most inconvenient moments. His theories about how to get along with the tribes in the jungle are highly enlightened and advanced. He may decide that the right thing to do with a bunch of hostile natives is to stroll among them casually, unarmed and trusting to their fundamental good nature. The problem is that the natives are not enlightened and advanced, and Crazy Inventor is lucky to escape with a whole skin.

People with Uranus in Ninth frequently seem to be so liberal and freethinking that they are completely lost. I have heard people with Uranus in Ninth being very profound and perceptive when they are talking theoretically. When it comes to action and the realities of their personal lives, all their knowledge goes out the window.

They are independent to a fault and often behave in ways that strike the observer as naive. They are following their star, and a pretty strange, science fiction kind of star it is!

♅ Uranus

10th House

Business Executive

Crazy Inventor as Chairman of the Board is the despair of his colleagues and the shareholders. We need to imagine him as the boss of a small electronics or microchip company. His genius created the company through his brilliant inventions. Now that he is the administrative head, he is a disaster. He has no business sense whatsoever and can't understand that tradition and routine are necessary. He keeps wanting to change such fundamental things as the production line and the accounting system, or to experiment with new management techniques. No one knows where they stand, and the company is on the brink of collapse.

People with Uranus in Tenth are often highly ambitious and have more restless energy than they know how to use. They want the prestige of a secure social position yet, at the same time, they half despise themselves for this desire, feeling that they should be above all that sort of thing. They don't like vagueness and abstract ideas. They are abrasive, wanting to get down to the nitty-gritty of a situation. Their ambivalence about their own ambition either turns them into dropouts or makes them twice as restlessly ambitious as anyone else. Heinrich Himmler and Henry Kissinger are examples of the second kind. William Blake, the eighteenth-century poet, is an example of the first. Actually, he was an ambitious dropout. He rejected conventional values and ideas, yet worked incredibly hard, writing, painting, and publishing his own works.

Uranus ♅

11th House

Social Worker

Being a Social Worker is one of the better opportunities for the Crazy Inventor. He is no good at all as far as dealing with the actual people goes, but at the planning level, he has the imagination and flair to solve problems that look insoluble. He can come up with big, break-through ideas and make them work. He might, for example, cut the heating bills for poor people by installing solar heating panels in their homes on government grants. Of course, this means he is in constant conflict with his bosses, who always think his ideas are impractical and unworkable at first.

People with Uranus in Eleventh tend to be intellectual and impersonal, though sometimes, as with D. H. Lawrence, they use their intellect to proclaim the need for freedom of feelings and instincts. They always have some kind of revolutionary, innovative ideas or programs. Authority is just a bad word to them; they have to be constantly challenging the status quo. If they are unable to exert much influence on anything, they can be terrible moaners, always complaining and never actually doing anything. They tend to be philosophical complainers, though, and will go on about the way the world is, rather than about the shortcomings of individual people.

These people place a lot of value on friendship, but they don't really relate to others as individuals. However, they are often excellent company because of their energy and unusual viewpoints.

♅ Uranus

12th House

Castaway

Crazy Inventor is not fazed by being marooned on a desert island. If he can't use the material technology he is used to, he will use mental technology. So he meditates and does yoga exercises until he is in complete control of his own mind and can perform magic. He is like Prospero in Shakespeare's *The Tempest*. He is able to command spirits of air who create good weather for him, spirits of earth who bring him food and drink, spirits of water who entertain him, and spirits of fire who inspire him to even greater efforts. He soon stops bothering about being rescued.

People with Uranus in Twelfth are, at the very least, highly sensitive and intuitive. They pick up impressions that most others don't notice. Generally, they have a more or less active interest in occult or "New Age" subjects. Only a few will be comfortable with this, and most Uranus in Twelfth people will make a big effort to seem conventional in public. Your Uranus in Twelfth friend may be an insurance salesman during the day and an astrologer or magician in his spare time.

Their sense that they can do some sort of magic can be an asset or a liability. Hitler had Uranus in Twelfth, and he used his "magic" for selfish and destructive purposes. Werner Erhard, the founder of *est*, used it in an attempt to bring enlightenment and a better life to others. It is always a dangerous gift, though, and Werner seems more recently to have created much trouble for himself. These people generally have more than their share of nervous tension and are liable to psychological and psychosomatic problems.

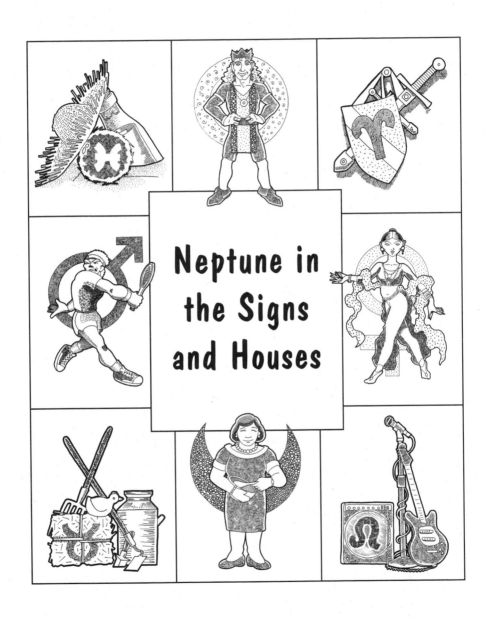

Neptune in the Signs and Houses

Neptune Ψ

1st House

Knight Errant

The Romantic Poet lives in a world of fantasies and ideals. As a Knight Errant, he loves the *idea* of riding around in shining armor, jousting with his fellow knights in noble and chivalrous combat, and rescuing beautiful damsels. The realities, that the armor is heavy and smelly, the blood and bruises of combat highly unpleasant, and that the damsel may turn out to be ungrateful for her rescue, shock him deeply. So he pretends they don't exist and goes on living out his dream of knights errant.

People with Neptune in First House never quite seem to get to grips with reality. It may not always *look* like that. Neptune is a planet of illusion and deception. Sometimes, people with Neptune in First can create such potent and appealing images of themselves that they impress others as capable and effective. But there is always some inner weakness in whatever image of potency they project. It may be drink or drugs or a heavy dependence on some other, often unacknowledged, person.

Most Neptune in First people, however, do actually seem to be dreamy and vague. They are often changeable and elusive. You never know quite where you are with them. You may come to what you think is a firm agreement with a Neptune in First person, only to find that they have understood things quite differently. They are perfectly sincere about it, and it is difficult to get mad at them, even though you want to.

♆ Neptune

2nd House

Farmer

The Romantic Poet imagines that being a Farmer will mean living in a country idyll. He sees himself perhaps sitting for hours tending a flock of sheep while he reads or composes poetry. A trifle more practically, he might see himself as part of a commune of fellow romantics, tilling the earth in a natural bond of fellowship. The actual mess of farm life and the back-breaking labor are enough to send him into a decline. He has to get drunk every day to face the life at all. He doesn't write any poetry either.

People with Neptune in Second often have very little ability to manage their personal affairs. They can be quite indifferent to money, yet of course, they need it. Their unwillingness to think about material realities can mean that they get involved in morally dubious, or illegal, or, at least, hand-to-mouth ways of earning a living. The lucky ones are those, like Dickens and Lewis Carroll, both with Neptune in Second, who can live by their imagination.

They often have a rather glamorous quality, and the sometimes ethereal and spiritual image they create can be sexually magnetic. There is a certain naiveté about these people that is both exasperating and appealing. Whether men or women, they all have a kind of "dumb blonde" personality tucked away somewhere.

Neptune ♆

3rd House

News Reporter

The realities of being a News Reporter are also irritating and restricting for the Romantic Poet. He dreams of writing articles and news stories that will inspire his readers, make them think about the meaning of life. Instead, he finds himself writing about the latest trade figures or the increase in crime statistics. He is disgusted and bored with the job. Everyone else acts as though the things they write about are vitally interesting. The Romantic Poet tries to pretend they are, but he finds the pretense very wearing.

People with Neptune in Third usually have a peculiar way of thinking about mundane realities. At their best, they will see the realities of day-to-day life as symbolic of deeper and more mysterious truths. This was the case with Carl Jung, the psychologist. More often, they will have some kind of chip on their shoulder.

They are too idealistic, even gullible. They get carried away by exciting ideas and projects, but don't think them through. Then they are disappointed when their technicolor fantasies turn out to be ordinary reality. These are the people who *always* expect the frozen food to be as good as the picture on the packet. They may complain about it, they may even make wry jokes about how gullible they are, but every time they see a new rainbow, they just *know* that this time it has the crock of gold at the end of it.

Neptune in the Signs and Houses   159

Ψ Neptune

4th House

Baby Sitter

At last the Romantic Poet has a job he can enjoy and do well. He is good at baby-sitting because he is half child himself and completely in tune with his charge. He knows exactly what to do to please the child and has a fund of fairy stories that he tells enchantingly. With the doors shut and the lights low, the Romantic Poet is able to create a world of warmth, love, and domestic happiness, rather like the atmosphere of a television commercial for detergent! If a fuse blows or the sink gets stopped up or the child becomes cranky, he is completely at a loss.

People with Neptune in Fourth usually live pretty much in a world of their own. It might be an illuminated, enlightened kind of world, in which they are able to communicate and share with others. An example of such a Neptune in Fourth is Werner Erhard. He was able to communicate something of his mystical vision of life to thousands of people through his *est* seminars. More often, the Neptune in Fourth person will harbor secret and unrealistic fantasies of security and domestic happiness.

The unreality of their fantasies makes Neptune in Fourth people vulnerable and oversensitive. They can get obsessively fixated on a particular goal or a particular person and, when the outer world never fulfills their dreams, they can become depressive and melancholy. They can get very involved in a cause or some offbeat subject like magic or depth psychology. No matter how outwardly active they may be, there is always some inner need motivating them.

Neptune ♆

5th House

Pop Star

The Romantic Poet is not really very good as a Pop Star. True, he looks handsome and magnetic and has a hypnotic voice, but he tries to be too spiritual and creative. He likes to sing songs with wistful and romantic lyrics full of obscure references. Although he seems to have everything going for him, he doesn't quite come across to the audience, and he ends up looking a wimp. He creates expectations in his audience that he doesn't fulfill. They go home disappointed, yet find it difficult to say exactly why.

People with Neptune in Fifth usually have a hint of something glamorous or mysterious about them. The mystery and glamour may be a little sleazy, but it still attracts others. The Neptune in Fifth person typically seems to be misunderstood. It's as if they are giving out a message that is quite different from what they think they are giving out. If you respond to the invitation this person is apparently offering, you are likely to find that some cross-up has occurred and you are at odds with them when everything appeared to be going smoothly.

It can work both ways. Human nature being what it is, what usually happens is that you are first impressed with the person, then disappointed; but you sometimes meet a Neptune in Fifth person who creates a poor impression and then turns out to be rewarding. Lord Byron had Neptune in Fifth. He created the image of being a moody loner and misanthrope, but was actually gregarious and loyal to his friends.

♆ Neptune

6th House

Doctor

Being a Doctor is difficult for the Romantic Poet. For one thing, he is much too impressionable. He feels the sufferings of his patients too keenly and is nervous about prescribing for them in case the drugs do more harm than good. Even worse, he is liable to think that he has every disease he has to treat, or is in danger of catching it. He is over-conscientious and works much too hard, not because he is a workaholic, but because he feels obliged to give himself endlessly to his patients. Pretty soon, he has to take a drink to keep himself going.

People with Neptune in Sixth are generally plagued with guilt feelings. They feel that a lot is expected of them and that they never quite match up to it. They overwork and get caught up in the Puritan Work Ethic. Often, they get so tired that they have no energy or attention left for anything else, and they seem cold and unappreciative. Although they work hard, they frequently doubt the value of what they have achieved and need a lot of boosting, though it is hard for them to respond to praise.

John Keats's chart is doubtful because we don't have the birth time, but he very likely had Neptune in Sixth. Even if he didn't, he really *was* a romantic poet who trained as a doctor! He had to give it up because he couldn't stand bleeding his patients. This is fairly typical of the Neptune in Sixth person. They have a strong desire to help and give service to others, yet some inner weakness makes them less than effective.

The Romantic Poet is too dreamy and too eager to please everyone to be a good Maitre d'. He can't stand upsetting people and so he won't turn anyone away because there are no tables available. He makes promises he can't fulfill, telling customers they will be seated in ten minutes when he knows there won't be a free table for at least half an hour. He often finds himself having to calm down two sets of customers, to both of whom he has promised the next vacant table. All this friction that he creates by his own lack of clarity and firmness would shred his nerves, but he spaces out and withdraws from it.

People with Neptune in Seventh are often personally impressive. When they are talking to you, they make you feel as though all they are interested in is you and your concerns. They give you their total attention and you go away confident that they will do what they said they would do. The catch is that the next person they talk to gets exactly the same treatment and the new encounter obliterates their previous agreements. They are rather like Neptune in First people except that you never have the feeling of knowing where you are with Neptune in First, whereas you think you know where you are with Neptune in Seventh.

It works the other way as well. People with Neptune in Seventh often find that those they are involved with turn out to be disappointing in some way, if not downright treacherous.

♆ Neptune

8th House

Private Eye

Being a Private Eye is much too sleazy and unpleasant for the Romantic Poet. He has seen plenty of Bogart movies so he knows how a Private Eye should behave. He buys a trench coat and a fedora, rents an office in a cheap part of town, keeps a bottle of bourbon in the file cabinet, and learns how to talk tough. He wouldn't be able to solve a case if he came across the murderer standing over a corpse with a smoking gun in his hand! Romantic Poet has great fantasies about being a Private Eye. Such clients as he might get end up in worse trouble than when they started.

People with Neptune in Eighth often make a great show of really getting down to the roots of things. They seem seriously committed to solving the problems of existence, but their commitment never goes below the surface.

A good example here is Alan Watts, who wrote copiously about Zen and other Eastern religions, and extolled the virtues of meditation and other yoga practices. The titles of some of Watts's books sound like the answer to everything you ever wanted to know. The contents stay on an unsatisfying intellectual level. According to his biographer, Watts probably never meditated in his life, yet he wrote as though he knew all about what can be achieved by meditation. With more self-insight than most Neptune in Eighth people, Watts described himself as "a genuine fake!"

Neptune in Eighth people talk big, mean well, and are utterly sincere. They just don't connect with what is actually going on.

The Romantic Poet leads his party of Explorers as though he were John Wayne starring in a movie. He doesn't make decisions; he strikes poses. When he is told that the party is lost or has run out of drinking water, he puts on a brave face and tells them to think positively. He is optimistic to the point of lunacy and refuses to deal with the question of how to think positively while dying of thirst or being eaten by cannibals. If he's lucky, the more practical members of the party will carry him through.

People with Neptune in Ninth often seem inspired by some kind of genius. They are able to conceive impressive, even grandiose, schemes and are so genuinely convinced about them that they fairly easily convince others. In order to carry out the schemes, the Neptune in Ninth person then resolutely shuts out and denies any conflicting realities. They are like Christian Scientists, denying that pain is real. The more strong-minded of them can generate a powerful self-righteous conviction that is very difficult to withstand. Margaret Thatcher, who was known in some quarters as The Iron Maiden, is an example.

Their platform always sounds good and is good, as far as it goes. They are idealistic and generous, champions of justice and compassion, but there is always a quality about them of being a hero or heroine of a school story or moral tale—slightly unreal.

♆ Neptune

10th House

Business Executive

As Chairman of the Board, the Romantic Poet makes a good figure-head, provided he has plenty of reliable people to do the real work. He goes in for impressive offices, chauffeur-driven limousines, and long business lunches in his private dining suite in the penthouse. He hasn't a clue about what his company really does, but he is superb at public relations. On television, he looks exactly the way a tycoon should look, and he has a gift for making apparently sincere and thoughtful speeches that brilliantly point up the issues facing the business community. It's all an impersonation, but done magnificently.

People with Neptune in Tenth have, above all, a gift for creating a powerful image. When I say "powerful," I don't necessarily mean that the person will come across as strong and capable. Depending on other things, they might create the image of being a feeble-minded layabout, but whatever it is, the image is striking. These are not people you easily forget, though you may not remember them with pleasure. Frank Sinatra, Aleister Crowley, and John F. Kennedy all have Neptune in Tenth. They are examples of people who create an image of power.

Unless there is something else in the chart to stabilize them, Neptune in Tenth people are not very reliable. The image can flicker in the wind a good deal, and they are often infuriatingly vague when you try to pin them down to details. They will sometimes reverse a stand they were taking only a few minutes before, apparently with no sense of anything odd.

Neptune ♆

11th House

Social Worker

As a Social Worker, the Romantic Poet is at least doing a job he can feel enthusiastic about. He wants to create a true fellowship of humanity and is full of passionately held convictions and schemes for improving the world. Needless to say, most of them are impractical and take no account of human nature. The Romantic Poet's colleagues and clients don't regard him very seriously. They know he means well, but they are liable to agree with him to his face and then do the opposite, and more sensible, thing behind his back.

People with Neptune in Eleventh are rather like those with Neptune in Sixth, except that they don't want to help others by doing things for them. They want to help by teaching other people how to think differently. They feel that humans would be better if they had richer and more spiritual aims. This may be true, but it is not a point of view that is very well received. The Neptune in Eleventh person feels he is talking to a brick wall and eventually shuts up.

Their friends find them infuriatingly ungrounded, elusive, and unwilling to be committed to specific arrangements. In turn, they discover that their friends are apt to be strange and not what they seem, seldom to be relied on in any kind of crisis. It is much the same as with Neptune in Seventh except that, for Neptune in Eleventh, the results are likely to be less damaging because they never really trusted the relationship anyway.

♆ Neptune

12th House

Castaway

Finally, the Romantic Poet has gotten away from all those tedious jobs that force him to deal with the messy and intractable physical world. He throws himself on the beach of his desert island with a heartfelt sigh of relief. Now he is in his element. He can spend all his time wandering lonely as a cloud over the island, talking to the animals, being nourished by the beauty of nature, and writing the marvelous poetry he hasn't had time for before. It is a touch lonesome, though, especially at night, when he is liable to lie awake wondering what all the eerie noises are.

People with Neptune in Twelfth are extremely sensitive to their environment. They need long periods of being alone or they are liable to get swamped by the feelings and needs of others. They are highly compassionate and are natural Good Samaritans, though the help they give sometimes takes strange forms and is not always appreciated by the recipient. And, as is the case with all the planetary positions that go with high sensitivity, Neptune in Twelfth people can suppress it and act very tough indeed. General Patton had Neptune in Twelfth and no one ever thought he was a soft touch. On the other hand, he was full of romantic ideas about being a soldier and was convinced that he had lived many previous military incarnations. This illustrates the tendency to unusual ideas and beliefs that Neptune in Twelfth people frequently have. These people often make good actors or, at least, behave in dramatic ways.

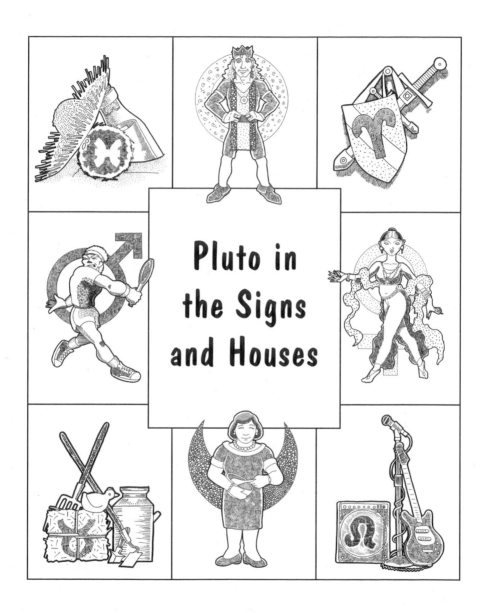

Pluto in
the Signs
and Houses

Pluto ♇

1st House

Knight Errant

The Magician doesn't stay a simple Knight Errant for long. He becomes king of the Knights Errant, using his magical powers to dominate his knights. Under his control, they are not so independent. They no longer go off on quests of their own, but do what the Magician wants them to. He molds them into a powerful army that, along with his magical power, is almost invincible. The Magician doesn't mix with his knights much. He prefers to live in a dark, lonely tower where he can perform his magic in secret. He's on the side of the good guys, but the bad guys are always trying to win him over.

People with Pluto in First always have a quality of power about them. There is a heavy, dark intensity in the way they meet the world. You will rarely find someone with Pluto in First who seems relaxed and casual. "Life is real! Life is earnest!" as far as these people are concerned. They *can* take a joke, as long as it is not about one of their many personal obsessions or ambitions.

They are frequently adventurous and have a great desire for experience of all kinds. Often, too, they have a lot of personal and sexual magnetism, which gets them into trouble as much as not because they don't really want to relate. They want to control, keeping at least seven-eighths of themselves deeply hidden and reserved.

♇ Pluto

2nd House

Farmer

The Magician always wants to dominate and control, no matter what job he has. So, as a Farmer, he will use magic to ensure that his crops and cattle thrive. He won't do the farm work himself, of course. He will have well-trained and well-paid laborers working for him. He can afford to pay top dollar, after all, with all that fairy gold in his cellars. With his magic, he can make even the most barren soil fertile.

People with Pluto in Second tend to be much concerned with the need to make money and enjoy the material world. They like to have the security of a lot of capital. One man with Pluto in Second who was making good money thought he was poor because he couldn't afford the best restaurants, theaters, nightclubs, clothes, and car, and save as well. He is fairly typical of the Pluto in Second person. Given his dilemma, most of them will do what he did and enjoy the material goodies rather than save. The writer Henry Miller had Pluto in Second. His books are about his personal experience and are described as "richly lusty and earthy."

In general, the Pluto in Second person will get thoroughly involved with life, usually to some kind of excess. They like thrills and sensations, and may choose some unsavory ways of getting them.

The Magician disdains being a News Reporter. If he must be in the news-paper business, he will be a proprietor. He runs the paper with a firm hand and insists on editorial control. The news that gets into his columns is all heavily slanted to reflect his view of the world and how it ought to be. Only opinions that agree with his own are allowed, but his own views are so wild, so deeply searching of the structure of society, that his viewpoint, though monolithic, is pretty radical.

People with Pluto in Third communicate in a heavy, massive, intense way. Werner Erhard and Carl Jung both have Pluto in Third. Anyone who has read one of Jung's books will know what I mean. He marshals every relevant fact he knows to make his point and half beats the subject to death with the sheer weight of material and ponderous writing. Similar things can be said of Werner Erhard. At the lowest level, these people can be insensitive buttonholers, backing you into a corner at a party and ham-mering you relentlessly with their conversation—or, rather, harangue.

With the low-rent type of Pluto in Third, the harangue will usually be about the way people in authority don't appreciate him and prevent him from getting where he should be. The average Pluto in Third person is not so extreme, but they all are serious all the time. They have no idea how to make small talk.

♇ Pluto

4th House

Baby Sitter

Having the Magician as a Baby Sitter is not an event the child will remember with much pleasure. For one thing, he is stern and rather creepy. If she starts acting sassy and won't go to bed on time, he will fix her with a hypnotic stare and she will be in bed and asleep before she knows what's happened. For the Magician, this is a rather trivial job, but he makes the best of it by using the time to educate the child. By the time he has finished with her, she has learned to doubt and question everything. She definitely does not believe in Santa Claus or the Easter Bunny.

People with Pluto in Fourth have a sense of being radically different from most of those around them. They pretty much write their own book of rules and often seem to spend their time trying to subvert the world about them. If they go really bad, they can be gangsters, crooked politicians, or unscrupulous tycoons. The better sort of Pluto in Fourth includes R. D. Laing, who attacked and subverted establishment psychiatry in the interests of a more humanitarian and patient-centered approach. Dickens is another example of someone actively concerned with reform and cutting away the roots of unenlightened and oppressive traditions.

The average Pluto in Fourth person probably won't seem all that radical. They will usually be extremely stubborn, though, sticking to a point of view or course of action no matter what.

When the Magician gets up in front of the microphone, he has no intention of entertaining anybody. Maybe he will do an act letting the audience know what it is like to be a concentration camp victim or to go insane. Whatever he puts over, there will be nothing comforting in it. Those of the audience who don't leave after the first few minutes will be riveted by the way the Magician transcends his subject matter and gives them a transforming and emotionally purging experience. Maybe he will perform an excerpt from a Greek tragedy, whose purpose was "to purge with pity and terror."

People with Pluto in Fifth probably shut down on the strangeness of this energy unless they are unusually creative or talented. Some of them use the energy destructively and become hell-raisers, getting drunk in public and smashing up a bar for an evening's pleasure.

Others may make radical discoveries, like Admiral Byrd, who was the first man to fly over the North Pole and later helped open up the Antarctic. He wrote a book about his experiences called *Alone*, and this well describes the Pluto in Fifth position. Indeed, they may be so alone they live entirely in an inner world and are autistic. Another Pluto in Fifth was Gustave Flaubert, the author of *Madame Bovary*. Described as a cheerless pessimist, Flaubert would work obsessively to produce a perfect piece of writing, sometimes spending hours over a single sentence. Most people with this position will repress the energy and who can blame them!

♇ Pluto

6th House

Doctor

As a Doctor, the Magician naturally wants to get to the deepest roots of his patients' troubles, so he specializes as a psychiatrist. With his magical powers, he is able to probe deeply into his patients' minds and reveal the deep traumas that are causing the problems. After that, it is up to the patients. Some are able to face the traumas and are healed. Others back away from them, repress them again, and may be worse than before. The trouble with the Magician's approach is that it is make it or break it. He is often harshly confrontational, more interested in attacking the disease than healing the patient.

People with Pluto in Sixth are often hard and demanding on themselves and on others. On this list, we have Freud, who was constantly demanding of his followers and couldn't bear anyone to disagree with his theories. These people usually work extremely hard and have such a bloodhound nose for detail that they lose sight of the main picture. One result of this is that they can get involved in labyrinthine projects of dubious morality or legality. An example here is John Dean, who served a prison sentence for his part in the Watergate conspiracy.

Perhaps the most usual characteristic of the Pluto in Sixth person is hard and obsessive work, always seeking to improve themselves and their methods. This frequently results in them gaining some measure of success—if never as much as they want.

As Maitre d', the Magician stands no nonsense from anyone. If a customer dares to complain, at the very least he will be hypnotized into eating sawdust and thinking it is a delicious gourmet meal. At the worst, he may be turned into a chicken and end up in the kitchen. The weird aura of power the Magician gives off is partly what attracts the customers. They like to kid themselves that they, too, are powerful enough to handle magic. Pretty soon, the restaurant becomes a cult place for people who like certain kinds of thrills. Others won't go within a mile of it.

People with Pluto in Seventh are apt to be extremely controlling in their relationships. They know what they want and what they want is what they get. Or else!! Perhaps champion of the Pluto in Seventh group is L. Ron Hubbard, founder of the Scientology cult, which is notorious for the severe control it exercises over its members. Pluto in Seventh people are usually combative, and they simply have no idea what the word "compromise" means. Any small disagreement is likely to be turned into a big stand on principles, which really means the Pluto in Seventh person is fighting for control.

This powerful need for control generally leads them into relationships with people who do not want to be controlled. Then the Pluto in Seventh person feels unappreciated. From their point of view, they are not controlling, they are being generous and concerned.

♇ Pluto

8th House

Private Eye

As a Private Eye, the Magician is unbeatable. He doesn't bother with mundane clues. He'll look into a crystal ball or conjure up a demon to tell him what he wants to know, and maybe catch the criminal as well. He lives in a lonely house by the edge of a marsh and prefers to take cases that have something supernatural about them. He is more of an exorcist than a Philip Marlowe-type of Private Eye. The Magician has a large army of spies and informers, both human and otherwise. He sits in the center of a web of power and intrigue where small manipulations will cause big effects.

Machiavelli, the notorious Renaissance statesman, had Pluto in Eighth. His name is associated with double dealing and the ends justifying the means, which often included treachery and cruelty. Winston Churchill and Margaret Thatcher are two more Plutos in Eighth. Both were able to handle a lot of power and to cope with making unpopular decisions. This position of Pluto produces the realist, the person who sees the world as harsh and tough, and who is prepared to be harsh and tough in order to deal with it.

Pluto in the Eighth is a placement the average person will tend to repress. There isn't room for many Machiavellis or even Thatchers, but the energy will usually manifest as having an eye to the main chance and a belief that most things can be accomplished by manipulation behind the scenes. The individual Pluto in Eighth person may not be in a position to do any manipulating on his own account, but he will be convinced that this is how things get done.

Pluto ♇

9th House

Explorer

The Magician is always in total control of any situation, and if he is going to lead a party of explorers, he will do it with maximum force. His party will be heavily armed and will operate in vehicles specially designed for the terrain. Being a deep-sea explorer in a bathysphere would appeal to him. Any trouble from the natives and the explorers will shoot first, with cannon and machine guns, and ask questions afterward. No obstacles will be allowed to get in the way of the expedition, and its aims will be accomplished efficiently and ruthlessly.

People with Pluto in Ninth tend to set major goals for themselves. They are adventurous and will have a go at anything, but they need to create a strong power base first. Frank Sinatra and John F. Kennedy are examples of Pluto in Ninth.

If the person is not able to create a sufficient power base, they are liable to be just restless and discontented. They throw themselves into plausible schemes that never quite work out. They are strongly intuitive, but not so good at grounding their intuitions and thinking things through, and they seldom take enough account of the effects of their actions on other people. Their enthusiasm can lead them to neglect the need for resources. If they go into business, they will either be undercapitalized or spend so much time getting capital together their enterprise never gets off the ground.

♇ Pluto

10th House

Business
Executive

As Chairman of the Board, the Magician is the complete tycoon—single-minded, ruthless, interested only in power and profits. He is like one of the "robber baron" nineteenth-century industrialists. Truly, he is a pluto-crat. His money doesn't talk, it shouts. Too often his dollars will tip the scale of some political or economic decision. The balance will always tilt to the advantage of himself and his company, of course. He is one of the rich who get richer. At least he enjoys his money and power, and doesn't pretend he is working for the good of humanity.

All people with Pluto in Tenth are power worshipers, either openly or secretly. Perhaps they don't know it themselves, but let them have a little power and their juices start running. They come alive and begin to feel they are *somebody* at last. It can be a dangerous addiction. Richard Nixon had Pluto in Tenth. He is an example of the lengths to which an out-of-control Pluto in Tenth power junkie will go to keep his fixes coming. Other examples are Lord Byron and Aleister Crowley, who also went to considerable lengths to keep themselves in power situations.

All three examples came to severe grief. Pluto in Tenth can be like Lucifer thrown out of heaven. Most people with Pluto in Tenth probably never get their hands on much power, but they hunger for it. This keeps them in a very uneasy relationship with anyone in authority. If they have any sense though, they will act with total integrity. Otherwise, a big fall will bring retribution.

Pluto ♇

11th House

Political Candidate

The Social Worker idea doesn't quite suit the Magician. Better to see him as a Political Candidate running for office on a radical, humanitarian platform. He will do away with poverty, racial discrimination, and street crime. He presents himself as having no image, being a plain, outspoken man who talks good common sense to the voters. His performance is mesmeric and he does influence a lot of people. He comes up with truly brilliant plans for reform, so simple and obvious that people kick themselves for not having thought of them before. How the plans will work out if the Magician gets elected is another matter.

People with Pluto in Eleventh are usually, in some way, crowd pleasers. They instantly know how to fit into their particular group, whatever that might be. They don't necessarily have radical views. The fact that they seem to focus, even embody, what their group thinks, feels, and wants, gives them an air of authority and certainty. It is not an authority that is truly earned, but they are normally very secure in it. However, they can become alarmed when someone voices opposite views. Generally, they take good care not to be around such people.

If you try to get Pluto in Eleventh people to define exactly where they stand on anything, they will become vague and elusive. They know where they stand, as long as they don't have to think about it.

ℙ Pluto

12th House

Castaway

The Magician doesn't get *marooned* on the desert island. He goes there on purpose to perform rituals that can be done only in secrecy and solitude. Away from the pressures of the world, the Magician on his island can best work for the good of humanity. His rituals call down the powers of light to bless and enlighten the world. He could equally well call down the powers of darkness for his own advantage, but he knows that would eventually go badly wrong for him. Nevertheless, he always has to fight against the temptation to use his magic to create personal glory and destroy his enemies.

People with Pluto in Twelfth are loners in some way, at least to the extent that they reveal only a thin layer of themselves. They may have large families, they may be completely social, but they still manage to keep a strong air of privacy. Most of them live entirely in their thin outer crust, never looking within because they are afraid of the chaos of feelings they might find if they did.

The hidden, swirling, chaotic energy has to come out somehow. These people are often gripped by irrational moods or convictions that something out of the ordinary is going to happen. They are frequently right, being so impressionable that they pick up tiny nuances and indications that others miss. The more conscious type of Pluto in Twelfth person will probably feel that he or she has to discover the deeper meaning of life, and will very likely be drawn to religion, the occult, or depth psychology.

Aspects

The Characters in Relationships

The planetary characters not only have to do two jobs each, they also have to get along with each other, and these relationships are shown by the aspects in the chart. To deal with aspects fully would take a book in itself. Each planet can make aspects to all the others, so there are forty-five possible combinations. Then the angle of the aspect makes a difference to the interpretation, and there are five main aspects that are traditionally regarded as important, plus several others that are thought to be not as powerful. If we were to deal with every possibility, we would have around two hundred sections of interpretations, which would make the book rather cumbersome.

Using the planetary characters makes it very easy to understand how aspects work, and we will deal with them quite briefly. The differences between kinds of aspects are much like the differences between signs and houses. They are definitely there, but they are subtle and we can afford to ignore them for our present purpose. All that matters, from our point of view here, is the two planets concerned.

The description of how the characters will get along can be modified, if you wish, according to the type of aspect. For example, we see that Moon and Mars, the Housekeeper and the Tennis Champion, don't get along well in any circumstances. However, if the aspect is a trine or sextile, we can imagine them doing their best to be polite and keep things under control. With the conjunction, they might be stiff and formal, and with the square and opposition, they could be having a blazing row. So, in interpretation, you could weight the description accordingly.

Aspects in the natal chart have a pecking order. When two planets make an aspect it is considered that the slower-moving planet affects the faster-moving planet, not the other way around. This is not true in predictive work, of course. The Magician, therefore, influences everybody else and the Housekeeper doesn't influence anybody. She has to take everything the others hand out. The standard practice in listing aspects is to do it with the faster planet first, except for the Sun. Being the center of the system, the Sun is always listed first.

Sun/Moon

The Housekeeper can't get on with her job because the King is hanging around all day being charming and charismatic. He keeps chatting with her, kissing her ears while she's washing the dishes, and asking why she hasn't ironed his shirts yet.

These people tend to be extravert, emotional, and dramatic. They are a little confused about identity and inclined to stick to familiar routines. They can be very restless, moody, and usually strongly sensual.

Sun/Mercury

The King is taking a not very intelligent interest in the Whiz Kid's computer. He doesn't have any idea about computers; he just wants to push buttons and play games. The Whiz Kid finds it difficult to stay polite.

These people will be restless, impatient, dogmatic. They tend to feel under a lot of pressure to express themselves and explain things, and often seem anxious and nervous.

Sun/Venus

The King can't keep his hands or eyes off the Temple Dancer. She is all a-flutter, not used to royal attention, excited, but wondering if she looks her best or is saying the right things.

These people will be amiable and affectionate, with a strong sexual nature, which may become passive and sentimental if thwarted. They are very aware of, and concerned about, their own image and are inclined to be flirtatious rather than committed.

Sun/Mars

Now the King is on the receiving end. The Tennis Champion is pestering him to open the next tennis tournament. The King is sympathetic, but he finds the TC's brash, hard-selling approach irritating, and this makes him argumentative.

These people will be assertive and aggressive, courageous and enterprising. It may not be easy to express so much energy fully, and sometimes a person is overloaded by it and seems emotionally paralyzed.

Sun/Jupiter

Favorite Uncle has called to see the King with a magnum of champagne and a box of Havanas. The King can relax and enjoy himself, swapping genial tall stories with his guest.

These people will be optimistic, generous, and fair-minded, interested in pleasure and good things rather than power or status. They may be a little extravagant and self-centered, but they know how to enjoy life.

Sun/Saturn

The King, reluctantly, has welcomed his Old Math Teacher, who has brought along his latest treatise on advanced math. What a bore! The King has to try to look interested while the old buzzard drones on about Boolean algebra and Riemann geometry.

These people will be rather self-disciplined, seeing things in terms of duty and responsibility rather than pleasure. They are emotionally inhibited and often feel inadequate, but are usually practical and resourceful.

Sun/Uranus

The King is fascinated by the Crazy Inventor's weird ideas and exciting schemes. He gets fired up about plans to modernize everything in the kingdom, much to the alarm of the more conservative inhabitants.

These people will be original with a strong sense of wanting to be different and to change things. They probably don't have much staying power, always wanting to move on to something new. They are overexcitable, hasty, and impulsive.

Sun/Neptune

The King always enjoys a bit of drama, so he likes listening to the Romantic Poet read his poems. He gets carried away by the poetry, hypnotized by mellifluous words and haunting images, and forgets about the realities and problems of his kingdom.

These people will tend to live in imagination and avoid confronting reality. They will be good at believing what they want to believe and may be susceptible to drugs or alcohol.

Sun/Pluto

The Magician is promising the King initiation into magical secrets and offers to teach him how to turn lead into gold. The King is strongly tempted, but nervous about what he may be getting into.

These people will, in one way or another, be strongly centered on achievement. They are often creative and will dream about being a leader and guiding the destinies of others.

Moon/Mercury

Computer Whiz Kid is hanging around the Housekeeper's kitchen, scrounging cookies and telling her she should automate the whole operation. This upsets and annoys her, but she tries to deal with him coolly and rationally.

These people will talk a lot and be very mentally active, always rehearsing and turning things over in their minds. They may be witty, grasping the essentials of an argument very quickly. They are highly critical, self-critical, and self-doubting.

Moon/Venus

The Housekeeper and the Temple Dancer have a lot in common. They sit around swapping recipes, eating chocolates, and talking about their love affairs. Housekeeper likes Temple Dancer, but is a little in awe of her beauty and glamour.

These people will be affectionate, sensitive, and gentle. Feelings usually have the upper hand. They need a lot of affection and reassurance, and may turn jealous or vengeful if they don't get them. There is a strong sexual and sensual nature.

Moon/Mars

Tennis Champion irritates the hell out of the Housekeeper. She can't stand his brashness and aggressiveness, and responds by being brash and aggressive herself.

These people will have high energy and a thrusting, courageous attitude toward life. They can't leave things alone, but always have to interfere, often in a tactless, insensitive way.

Moon/Jupiter

Favorite Uncle has taken the hardworking Housekeeper out on the town and is showing her a good time. Dinner, theater, and a nightclub afterward are just what she needs to make her feel good.

These people will be sociable and outgoing, usually kind, helpful, and considerate. They may also be extravagantly emotional or sentimental, and inclined to sample a lot of experiences without much discrimination.

Moon/Saturn

The OMT is giving the Housekeeper a lecture on how she should do her job. Everything he says is right in theory, even if it isn't always workable in practice, but the Housekeeper can't find the words to defend her side of the case.

These people will be cautious and careful in expressing themselves. Others can easily make them feel inadequate and inferior. They tend to be private and withdrawn, and to feel safer with familiar routines.

Moon/Uranus

The Crazy Inventor makes the Housekeeper feel very nervous indeed. She depends on habits, routines, and rituals to get her job done, and he is telling her she should scrap everything and rethink it. Some of what he says excites her, but mostly she is afraid of it.

These people feel as though they ought to be original and freewheeling, and will attempt to be, though with some reluctance. They are potentially very creative and inventive, though jumpy and capricious, with a lot of tension.

Moon/Neptune

The Housekeeper loves talking to the Romantic Poet and listening to him read his poetry. She especially likes the way he idealizes women, and his sensitivity brings out her maternal feelings.

These people tend to withdraw into their inner worlds a good deal, and are idealistic and oversensitive. They will be inclined to be passive and resigned to their "fate," and are liable to self-deception.

Moon/Pluto

The Housekeeper is partial to a little magic herself, so she gets along quite well with the Magician. The problem is that, if she spends too much time in his company, she becomes obsessive and loses some of her gentleness and compassion.

These people will be highly emotional and intense, though perhaps not obviously. In fact, they will tend to block and control their energies because they feel too powerful and disturbing. They are more influenced by inner feelings than by outer circumstances.

Mercury/Venus

The Temple Dancer is doing her level best to seduce the Computer Whiz Kid. He is experiencing sensations he never got from his computer. He doesn't know how to handle them, but he does know that he enjoys them.

These people will be agreeable and charming, taking everything personally, and are inclined to flatter and be too willing to please. They don't think very clearly or logically because they want to know only what their desires and feelings tell them.

Mercury/Mars

Computer Whiz Kid is tremendously impressed by the Tennis Champion. He is in awe of the TC's macho manner and dedication to winning. The Whiz Kid tries to be as much like his hero as possible, becoming even more aggressively logical and factual than usual.

These people think and speak in a rapid, forceful way, cutting through what they see as side issues. They may be deliberately sarcastic or satirical, and can be irritable, witty, and extremely restless, with no tact at all.

Mercury/Jupiter

Favorite Uncle is talking to the Computer Whiz Kid about the broad social, cultural, and philosophical implications and applications of computers. The Whiz Kid doesn't really understand it, but it sounds impressive and he gets fired up with some vague and impractical ambitions.

These people will generally be optimistic, inclined to take the broad view and not bother about details. They'll also be inclined to misjudgments, seeing problems as bigger or smaller than they really are.

Mercury/Saturn

The Old Math Teacher and the Computer Whiz Kid get along pretty well. The Old Math Teacher is full of ideas for improving software. Under his influence, the Whiz Kid becomes even more efficient and dedicated than before.

These people will take pride in being clear and realistic. They have good concentration and get straight to the point of an issue. They think profoundly and are not afraid to deal with difficult problems, but they can get too narrowly focused, unable to see the wood for the trees.

Mercury/Uranus

The Whiz Kid doesn't have very much stability to begin with. Under the influence of the Crazy Inventor, he becomes completely unhinged. He may get into saving the world, changing human nature, or traveling in time—all by computer control.

These people will be excitable, nervous, restless. They get very frustrated and tense because they feel that no one appreciates their brilliant and original ideas. They do have real talents for innovation, but trip themselves up by being too eccentric or extremist.

Mercury/Neptune

The Computer Whiz Kid has no idea what the Romantic Poet is all about. They don't live in the same universe. The Poet wears the Whiz Kid out— his brain goes mushy, he can't think clearly, and his imagination goes on the rampage.

These people will have strong intuitions and imagination, but may find it difficult to express their ideas. They are easily distracted and bothered by worries and vague fears, especially when they don't understand what's going on.

Mercury/Pluto

The Whiz Kid finds the Magician pretty scary. He reckons himself a strict nuts-and-bolts man, and the Magician's talk of strange powers beyond the realm of reason alienates him. He defends himself by refusing to listen, asserting his own view of the universe.

These people will usually speak and think in an intense and purposeful way. They will often be concerned with fundamental things and can be very opinionated and critical, not giving others a fair hearing.

Venus/Mars

Tennis Champion is coming on to Temple Dancer in a big way, using all his ruthlessness and drive to get her into bed. She is accustomed to being the one to make the moves. TC's approach excites her too much and throws her off balance.

These people will usually have a very strongly developed sexual drive. They are not generally very sensitive or tactful because the force of their own needs blocks out awareness of what other people want. There is generally too much emphasis on action, sexually, and not enough on feeling.

Venus/Jupiter

Favorite Uncle is exactly the kind of experienced, easy-going older man the Temple Dancer can really go for. He lets things take their own pace and she blossoms under his influence.

These people will operate mostly by feelings, will be big-hearted, sociable, charming, and popular. They are extravagant and expect too much, but they have a genuine "talent" for happiness.

Venus/Saturn

The Old Math Teacher is lecturing the Temple Dancer about her way of life. He tells her she should stop thinking about pleasure, love, and sex and be more serious, disciplined, and responsible. He goes on so much she begins to doubt her own worth and becomes timid and withdrawn.

These people will be inhibited and reserved, finding it difficult to give or receive love. All creative energies are blocked or at least severely hindered. Often, these people dislike being touched and can be unfeeling.

Venus/Uranus

Crazy Inventor is so wild and weird that Temple Dancer is completely dazed by him. He wants to turn her on to heights of sexual ecstasy she has never even heard of. She gets caught up in the excitement of his promises and loses her sense of practical reality.

These people will be very excitable, wanting a lot of drama and sensation in relationships, with the result that most ordinary ones can seem a little drab. They are always liable to sudden turn-offs as well as enthusiasms. Casual and informal, they can be intimate without being committed.

Venus/Neptune

The Temple Dancer is entranced by the Romantic Poet. She loves to hear him talk and read his poems. She gets into it so much she loses herself in a beautiful dream-world.

These people will be very idealistic and romantic, at heart if not in overt behavior. They are usually unrealistic about love and sex, and so liable to much disappointment. Much too impressionable, they may attract people who behave badly or unreasonably.

Venus/Pluto

The Magician teaches the Temple Dancer some powerful magic that enables her to control and increase her sexual energies. She becomes even more seductive and magnetic than she was to start with.

These people will have a strong sex drive, usually with a lot of personal magnetism, unless the energy is repressed. If it is, they may seem quite formal and rigid.

Mars/Jupiter

Tennis Champion enjoys being with Favorite Uncle, who encourages him and gives him useful tips on psyching himself up to win and spotting the weaknesses of his opponents. The Champion is twice as confident after one of these sessions.

These people will have a high success potential and be enthusiastic, optimistic, and generous. They can get results and are willing to be open to new ventures and ways of thinking, but they tend to overreach themselves, which can cut down their achievements.

Mars/Saturn

The Old Math Teacher keeps on and on at the Tennis Champion about the need for discipline and hard work, as if the TC wasn't working hard enough already. Pretty soon, the Champion is training and working incessantly, not allowing himself any pleasures or time off.

These people can be very precise, disciplined, and controlled, but also too harsh and demanding of themselves and others. Frustrated sexual energies may turn to coldness or even cruelty. Usually hard working, they have great powers of endurance.

Mars/Uranus

The Crazy Inventor is full of ideas about "power tennis," using Zen techniques, special diets, and programs of visualizing winning and making perfect shots. The Tennis Champion goes berserk for it and becomes even more individualistic and extremist.

These people will rely too much on techniques and technology and may, at heart, be quite insecure. They can be compulsive overachievers, very courageous and original, but liable to mess things up by being hasty and premature.

Mars/Neptune

The Tennis Champion can't get along with the Romantic Poet at all. He wants to talk about winning and pounding an opponent into the ground, and the Poet says, "Yes, but is there Truth and Beauty in it?" Eventually, the Tennis Champion gives up and goes to sleep.

These people will find it difficult to act decisively and assertively. It's hard for them to know what they really want, and they tend to get their way by creating a kind of benevolent fog around any issue. They are often lethargic unless there is a good creative outlet for the imagination.

Mars/Pluto

The Magician convinces the Tennis Champion that he must deliberately cultivate his will. The TC spends hours in deep meditation and gets fanatically caught up in a philosophy of "making his life work."

These people will be forceful and uncompromising, knowing what they want and going all-out to get it. They have steamroller personalities and want to solve all problems by force and effort. There is little real awareness of others.

Jupiter/Saturn

The Old Math Teacher has cornered Favorite Uncle in the bar of the club to which they both belong. The OMT is complaining and taking a pessimistic view of life. Favorite Uncle, who is tolerant enough to listen to anything, gets depressed and bored, but can't get away.

These people usually have a lot of tension and inhibition. They feel they have to advance cautiously and keep a low profile. Success comes to them through patience and endurance rather than by being venturesome.

Jupiter/Uranus

Favorite Uncle is always open to new ideas, and Crazy Inventor gets him wound up and enthusiastic. Before Favorite Uncle knows what has happened, he has invested money in one of the Inventor's crazier schemes.

These people will have an eye for the main chance, ready to grasp opportunities as they come along. They tend to see themselves as lucky, and they can be very extravagant. They may be rolling stones, impulsive, and always trying something new.

Jupiter/Neptune

Favorite Uncle and the Romantic Poet get along very well. Favorite Uncle has a large poetic streak in him anyway. The two of them sit up all night, getting drunk, singing songs, and telling tall stories.

These people are always expecting something to turn up, that the lucky break could come any time. They can't resist a gamble, and spend more than they can afford on lottery tickets and horses.

Jupiter/Pluto

Favorite Uncle is very ready to be impressed by the Magician's talk of strange powers. Under this influence, though, Favorite Uncle is apt to lose sight of the easy-going, tolerant part of himself and become unduly expansive.

These people will have strong desires for power and leadership, and need to do things in a big way. They are usually sincere and frank, possibly to the point of being rude.

Saturn/Uranus

For the first time, the Old Math Teacher has met someone who is not intimidated by him. Crazy Inventor calls the OMT a dreary old stick-in-the-mud. The Old Math Teacher is deeply shaken by such lack of respect.

These people will have a lot of tension and anxiety, feeling as though their foundations have been kicked away. They are prone to sudden swings in moods and failures of energy, but they also have a great capacity to keep going, if only in a plodding way.

Saturn/Neptune

The Romantic Poet refuses to take logic and reason seriously, so the Old Math Teacher has no way to get at him. The Poet weaves his dreamy spells. The OMT doesn't entirely succumb to them, but he feels as though he's wandering in a mist.

These people often have a feeling of confusion, of not enough structure and solid ground in their lives. They are liable to vague fears and can get involved in rather dubious schemes, which they usually mess up in some way.

Saturn/Pluto

The Old Math Teacher is impressed by the Magician. He recognizes that the Magician is talking about a higher form of logic, which his training in mathematics helps him to partly understand.

These people can drive themselves very hard, but often find that something continues to elude them, and they do not quite get the result they were after. All the same, they can sometimes do the "impossible." They generally like to go it alone and resent help from others.

Uranus/Neptune

The Crazy Inventor finds the Romantic Poet even crazier than *he* is! The Poet opens the Inventor up to even wilder possibilities. He starts working on invisibility and visiting parallel universes.

These people will tend to be impractical and otherworldly. They are easily blown off course by new developments and are likely to get into a lot of crises. They will also have periods of lack of drive and vitality.

Uranus/Pluto

The Inventor is completely captivated by the will power, strength, and dedication of the Magician. (It's like Mercury and Mars again.) The Inventor is soon working thirty hours a day to make his ideas reality.

These people will be very impatient with things as they are, wanting to change and reform them. They are inclined to be intolerant, ruthless, and inconsiderate. Once they are set on a course of action, they won't give it up.

Neptune/Pluto

Poetry is all very well, the Magician tells the Romantic Poet, but he should take it a stage further and actually manifest in reality the gods, nymphs, and fabulous creatures that he writes about. The Poet can't resist this idea and soon his house is filled with mythological beings.

These people will tend to get locked into the pursuit of unusual goals and ambitions, seeking strange, other-worldly experiences. They can create powerful images and are likely to be concerned with inner exploration.

The Strength of Aspects

In using aspects, one has to remember that they are not equally powerful. The aspects made by the faster-moving planets will be the ones with the most effect, and which should be readily observed in a person. All aspects made by the Sun, Moon, Mercury, Venus, and Mars should have noticeable effects. Aspects of Jupiter and Saturn with each other, and with the three outer planets, may be less obvious and have more of a background influence.

The last three aspects, Uranus/Neptune, Uranus/Pluto, and Neptune/ Pluto, are comparatively rare. When they do form, they will stay in place for years. Everyone born since 1940 has a Neptune/Pluto sextile, but not many will have the characteristics described. When they do, it will be because the planets are specially emphasized in other ways—by being connected with the Sun, Moon, Ascendant, or Midheaven, usually. These aspects of the outer planets should be noted, but in most charts, can be ignored for practical purposes.

Midpoint Aspects

The planetary characters can be used whenever aspects are being formed. They can be used, for example, for understanding midpoint pictures. Let us say we have Saturn = Sun/Venus, which means that Saturn is aspecting the midpoint of Sun and Venus. To interpret the midpoint picture, we see the two planets that form the midpoint as being in a relationship of some kind, and the third planet as influencing this relationship.

In the example we have taken, the King and the Temple Dancer are intent on having a good time, and the Old Math Teacher is doing his best to spoil it and break them up. If it had been Jupiter = Sun/Moon, the Favorite Uncle would be encouraging the pair.

Aspects by Transit or Progression

The more obvious area in which the characters can be used is that of prediction. Planets making aspects by transit, progression, or solar arc direction can be treated in the same way as aspects in the natal chart. One simply sees the transiting or progressed planet as having come for a visit.

The pecking order that applies to natal aspects does not apply here, of course. The visiting planetary character is seen as affecting the natal one, so, for example, with progressed Moon aspecting Pluto, the Housekeeper is disturbing the Magician, not the other way around.

When working with transits or progressions, it is important to consider not just the two aspecting planets, but the whole complex of sign, house, and natal aspects that is being stimulated. Suppose we have Mercury in Sagittarius and Sixth House, square Saturn, and trine Jupiter. Here's the Computer Whiz Kid working on one level as a foreign correspondent or explorer, which he does well. The Old Math Teacher keeps giving him a hard time, no matter what he does, while Favorite Uncle helps him out as much as he can. Along comes a Mars transit. The Tennis Champion comes to stay for a while and this is something else the Whiz Kid has to cope with.

The question is, what's going to be affected by the visitor's presence the most—Whiz Kid's personality, his job as foreign correspondent, his job as a doctor, his relationship with Favorite Uncle, or his relationship with the OMT? The answer is that one doesn't know until it happens.

The one-on-one delineations of transits or progressions that appear in books or computer interpretations are necessarily incomplete. They assume the effect of the visit will be entirely on the personality of the natal planetary character, but the effect can show in any of the factors, or perhaps in all of them. I've even known the effect of a transit to show up mainly in the affairs of the house where the planet ruling the house of the aspected planet was. In this example, with Mercury in Sagittarius, the sign on the cusp could be Scorpio and the effect of the transit might show up in whatever house Mars occupies, independently of the fact that Mars is the aspecting planet.

This kind of complication is very difficult to grasp when you are thinking of the chart in the usual way, but it is much easier to get a hold on using the characters and jobs.

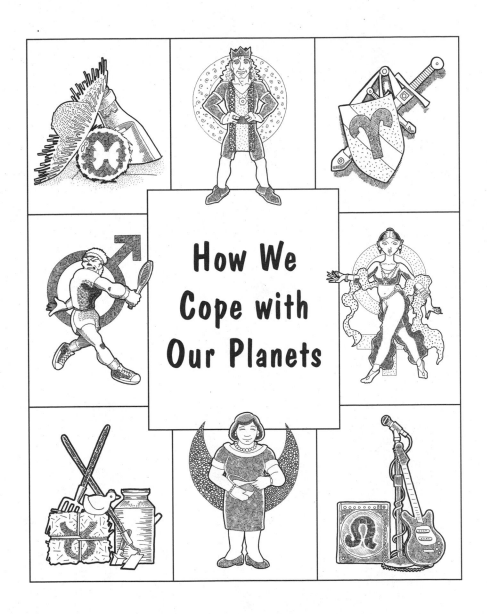

How We Cope with Our Planets

Coping with the Characters in Your Life

Without particularly stressing the point, we have so far been talking as though the planets exist as psychological forces within ourselves. In the model presented in this book, the planetary characters are something like middle managers in an organization. They get their instructions from some higher level; each one is assigned a couple of jobs to do and a certain number of the other planets that he or she has to relate to. The effects of the planets doing these tasks are a person's thoughts, feelings, behaviors, sensations, and general awareness of identity.

In this sense, we can see our personalities as being like the workers of the organization. They do what their immediate bosses tell them to do without understanding the policies behind their instructions. This level of being is the sort of non-reflective way in which we usually find ourselves dealing with the world. Much of our time is spent in simply coping with situations that arise or working to create situations and things we want.

It is only in periods of meditation or reflection that we become aware of the slightly deeper motivations that underlie our surface behavior and feelings. As I have suggested, one of the main values of thinking of our charts in terms of the images presented in this book is that it gives us access to this realm of inner motivation and so creates opportunities to understand our way of being and to change it if we want to do so.

In terms of the birth chart, this "workforce" that directly interacts with the outside world can be seen as the cusps of the houses. We are now shifting our perspective on what the houses mean, no longer seeing them as jobs the planetary "middle managers" have to do, but as ways in which we cope with and organize the tasks that our middle managers give us. At this level, we can think in the traditional concrete ways about the houses. The signs on the house cusps show how we express the inner planetary energies in our way of being in the world. The idea of signs as being jobs can be extended to this level.

For example, the Second House refers to material resources and values. If you have, let us say, Capricorn on the cusp of the Second House, it works to say that you will deal with money matters and personal values as if you were a business executive. That is, in this area of your life, you will more or less unconsciously fall back on qualities of prudence, ambition, status, and so on. If you have Leo on the Second House, you will play this role as if you were a pop star. You will have a tendency to use your possessions and resources to impress other people and gain their good-will, and you will most likely be generous and extravagant with your personal finances.

It would be cumbersome to try to give delineations for every possible combination of sign and house, and not really necessary. All you have to do to check the workability of the idea is to go around your own chart and see if it makes sense to say that you act, or at least have a kind of image of yourself, as a knight errant in one house and a maitre d' in the opposite house, as a conservative farmer in one area and a radical social worker or politician in another. Suitable meanings for the houses in this context are:

House	Meanings
First	Your general attitude
Second	Money, personal values, and resources
Third	Beliefs; the way you communicate, think, and speak
Fourth	Home, roots, and personal identity
Fifth	Creative self-expression
Sixth	Routine matters and health
Seventh	Relationships, other people in general
Eighth	Sexuality and other close involvements
Ninth	Religious/philosophical ideas
Tenth	Ambition and status
Eleventh	Functioning in groups
Twelfth	Solitude and introspection

In assessing the signs on the cusps, it is important to take into account the ruler of the sign. To go back to the previous examples, with Capricorn on the Second, the "business executive" effect will be less if Saturn, which rules Capricorn, is in Pisces or the Twelfth House, or some other area where the Old Math Teacher does not cope very well. Similarly, for Leo on the Second, the "pop star" effect will be less if the Sun, which rules Leo, is in Libra or Seventh, or some other place where the King has an uncongenial job. Aspects come into this as well. The straightforward effect of the sign on the house will also be modified by the aspects the sign ruler makes. However, this is getting into very subtle areas of interpretation, where your own personal skill and experience in chart reading will have to be your guide rather than anything that can easily be put into a book.

The Meaning of the Ascendant

Generally, the Ascendant, the sign on the cusp of the First House, is considered the most important of all the signs on house cusps. It seems, more than any other, to synthesize or summarize our outward reaction to the tasks we get from our planetary "middle managers." The exact meaning of the Ascendant is far from easy to define. It is a kind of half-intuitive, half-empirical way in which we learn to present ourselves to the world. It is the "act" we put on for other people, partly as a result of our sense of our inner potentials, partly through experience of what works. It is not usually a conscious act, though. It is more or less automatic, but we can become aware of it and so modify it to some extent.

What was said earlier about the rulers of the house cusps applies, of course, to the Ascendant. Aries rising, for example, will usually be bold and confident, but if Mars, which rules Aries, is in a difficult sign, say Cancer, Libra, or Pisces, or the corresponding houses, or is in aspect to Saturn or Neptune, which will have a depressing effect on Mars, the person will be more subdued than you would expect from the Ascendant alone. Bearing all these things in mind, we can do a quick run through the list of the twelve possible Ascendants.

Aries

These people come on to the world in a big, confident, challenging manner. They like to keep moving, are always up and doing something, and are often involved in battles and controversies. Above all, they are enterprising. They want to be *first* in everything, at the expense of being *best* if necessary, and they will push themselves forward to go for what they want without hesitation. They're not as secure as they look, though. The fast action is often like someone jumping onto a moving train—they won't be able to do it if they stop to think.

Taurus

These people create the impression that they have everything completely settled and worked out, and that there is no further need to get excited about anything. They like to stay in familiar surroundings and get very uncomfortable if their beliefs or opinions are challenged. *Solid* is the word for them, with all its implications. These people can be boring, but also reliable. Usually, they are gentle, but don't let that fool you into thinking that they don't pack a punch.

Gemini

Picture a butterfly doing a standup comedy act and juggling at the same time and you've got an idea of the Gemini-rising person. They love to talk. It might be empty prattle or serious discourse about the meaning of life, but the words will keep flowing. Don't expect to be able to pin these people down. They will be your best friend one minute and have forgotten who you are the next. It's not that they're callous, just too interested in everything to stay with anything for very long.

Cancer

These people have an air about them that is a curious mixture of being outgoing and, at the same time, wary. It's something like a kitten who's not sure if the tidbit is safe to eat, or maybe like the gunman in a western coming forward but listening for a suspicious sound behind him. You will never really get to know the Cancer-rising person. They always keep something in reserve. This often makes them attractive, with the air of having an intriguing secret.

Leo

Leo-rising people come on big, sunny, and usually benevolent. They are a bit like Aries rising except not so pushy, because they don't expect any opposition. Aries fights to get to the top; Leo expects everyone to acknowledge that it is his or her rightful place! They often have a kind of "star quality" about them that enables them to go places with sometimes quite mediocre talent. If they have *real* talent, the sky's the limit. These people expect, and usually get, a lot of attention. In return, they are generous with their time, energy, and money, but not so generous with their feelings. Leo rising loves an audience, but doesn't care for intimacy.

Virgo

These people are a little like Taurus rising to the extent that they give the impression of having everything worked out. But where people with Taurus rising are happy about their world, those with Virgo-rising have a hunted look that comes from the knowledge that they, personally, have to hold it all together. *Defensive* about sums up Virgo rising people. They won't do anything without having a good reason—or, at least, a rationalization—for it. Some of them look so well-groomed as to be scarcely human. Others find this too much and cultivate the scruffy look.

Libra

People with Libra rising are reasonable, well-balanced, and have an answer for everything. They may make you want to scream or hit them. Frequently, there is a sort of casual charm that lets you know the Libra-rising person is a nice guy and, at the same time, keeps you at arm's length. Actually, they are suppressing a lot of anger, and though they genuinely dislike hurting anyone, if they get too twisted they can be ruthless. Both Hitler and Churchill had Libra rising.

Scorpio

Heavy. Very heavy! These people go at life with a powerful determination. Everything is *serious* with them; they don't mess around. There is a kind of brooding, sexual quality about their presence that can be attractive or disturbing, depending on whether it turns you on or not. Underneath the bulldozer approach, these people are pretty scared. They go around saying "Boo!" to everyone else so that nobody will say it to them first.

Sagittarius

Sagittarius-rising people can be great complainers and layers down of the law. This contrasts oddly with the buoyant and optimistic way they carry on at other times. They usually have an open, even twinkly, quality about them, which makes the complaining and dogmatism even more jarring. They have big plans and they do get on with them. It doesn't all stay in the head. They love to lecture and they hate having to admit they might have been wrong about anything.

Capricorn

Capricorn-rising people look as if they have all the cares of the world on their shoulders. Often they do. People with Capricorn rising feel responsible for everything that's wrong and obliged to put it right. They have a big social conscience. They are the ones who will mention famine in Ethiopia at the dinner party when everyone else is falling about laughing. This is a suspicious group, even more defensive than Virgo. Paying any one of them a compliment is very hard work.

Aquarius

These are the space cadets. They go through life full of zest and enthusiasm, but slightly out of synch with everyone else. Often, they are just plain ornery. They will talk a lot. They love to discuss things, but it's hard to get them to actually do anything. Usually, they are very fast thinkers and quick on the uptake. Their problem is that they think they know all about something when they have grasped it only intellectually. This makes them exasperatingly detached and aloof.

Pisces

It is difficult to describe people with Pisces rising, but they have a sort of soft droopiness about them, even the ones who talk and act tough. They are painfully sensitive and intuitive, though many of them protect themselves by being cynical and taking a well-publicized interest in macho activities. They are helpful and supportive when other people are in trouble, and philosophical and reticent about their own problems. Having said that, though, there is a variety of people with Pisces rising that will fairly hose you down with their worries and anxieties. Most of them are too sensitive to your feelings to do this, however.

Appendix A

Working with the Characters

To get the most from this book, you need to learn how to become aware of your body and the feelings it contains. These feelings are often vague and subtle, and we pay no attention to them, yet they are the areas where real change in one's personality and life can occur. Learning to sense your body is a skill that takes time and patience to acquire, but it is well worth the trouble for the rewards it can bring, especially when it used with the images presented in this book.

Most of us live lives that are pressured to some degree or another. We are very largely caught up in the external world. There is always some job to be done or some fascinating entertainment to explore or something unpleasant to be coped with. It is seldom that we even think about taking time to explore our inner space. Many people would regard doing so as odd or eccentric.

Figuring something out about yourself by some kind of analysis, astrological or otherwise, doesn't result in real change. You can choose to modify your behavior, but the feelings that prompt the behavior are not affected. For example, if you have Jupiter in Aries, you might be made aware by a chart reading that you have a tendency to boast a little too much, so you can keep an eye on yourself, and when you find yourself embarking on a tall story, stop it. But the underlying feeling of *wanting* to let people know how good you are is not diminished, and in fact, you are liable to feel rather restrained. The key to real change lies in locating the expansive desire as a body-feeling and listening to it. You don't argue with it or insist that it should change. You have a dialogue with the feeling and allow it to become more assimilated into your life.

To get acquainted with your body, use the following technique. Allow yourself twenty minutes or half an hour at first. Later, with practice, you will be able to get in touch with your body-feelings almost immediately, but as I've said, this is a *skill* that needs to be learned. Everybody can learn it, but some people will learn faster than others.

Get comfortable, take a few breaths, and say to yourself, "I am now making friends with my body." Say this out loud if possible. You may be so out of touch with your body that you find at first that your body doesn't think much of the idea. After all, if somebody once close to you had persistently neglected you for years, you'd be suspicious if they suddenly started acting friendly! If you like, you can say something on the lines of, "I'm sorry we've been such bad friends, but let's start to get together again." See if you feel any response. What I mean by response is a vague, unclear feeling, a sort of aura of feeling in your body. I can't put it any more definitely than that because we are talking about something that is, of its nature, indefinite and inarticulate. We are persistently conditioned by our culture to believe that if we can't be clear and articulate about something, it is not worth bothering about. This is an attitude we have to put aside if we want to create real change in our lives.

The next step is to go through your body and ask yourself what's going on there. Start with your head and work down. See what's happening inside your skull. How does the back of your neck feel? What's going on in your throat? Remember, you're not looking for something you can easily put into words.

Carry on down. See what your chest has to tell you, your heart, solar plexus, abdomen, genitals, legs, and feet. You might come up with something like, "Well, there's a kind of foggy feeling in my skull, sort of like cotton wool. There's some tightness in my neck and shoulders, and my throat feels a bit closed up. I don't get much feeling at all from my chest, but there's a sort of faint happy feeling in my heart, like some good memory I can't quite call to mind. My solar plexus feels fluttery. There's some kind of excitement in my abdomen that I'm a little afraid of. My genitals seem completely numb, and my legs and feet feel kind of tensed up."

Whatever you find, even if it is a blank, say something like, "Hello, I know you're there. We'll get together again soon." This step is *extremely* important. Do it even if you get nothing at all and the whole process seems silly. In such a case, feeling silly is the feeling you need to start with, so say hello to that. In other words, whatever you get is what you need to explore, even if it's nothing.

Usually, it is easiest to find these vague feelings in the throat, chest, or abdomen, so you may do best to check those areas out first.

When you have developed some skill in sensing body-feelings, you can use it to work with the planetary images. Suppose you have Moon in Gemini and you find that you spend a lot of time running around like a blue-tailed fly, starting jobs and not finishing them, and generally being hyperactive. You decide you want to do something about this and be calmer. Or it may be that you recognize something else about yourself from the delineation of Moon in Gemini in this, or some other, book. In this book, I have treated the conventional delineations as being *symptoms*, the cure for which lies in working with the characters. That's why the delineations are often not particularly flattering. They are not meant to boost the ego. They are meant to encourage you to take a good look at whatever might be preventing you from living a full and happy life.

Read the description of the Housekeeper working in a news room and imagine how she feels, remembering that her nature needs a quiet, placid kind of job. Get the sense of what it is like for her and see if you can locate that feeling in your body after doing the body-sensing routine. See if there's a word to describe how the Housekeeper feels. It might be "fragmented" or "crazy" or something like that. Whatever is right for *you* is what matters. Then just sit with the feeling, as you might sit silently listening to a friend telling you about a problem with his or her job.

At some point, some kind of wordless shift will happen and you will feel better, even though the problem may seem as big as ever. Whether or not a shift does happen, thank the Housekeeper for being with you, and then get on with your life. At intervals, repeat the whole process until you can see some definite change in your behavior and feelings. A particularly good time to do this process is when your natal Moon is being transited by some planet. However, there's no need to wait for a transit.

The same technique is used for aspects you want to work with. How does the Temple Dancer feel about being with the Old Math Teacher who's boring her and telling her she should get a grip on herself and not be so sexual? Locate the feeling in your body and allow the Temple Dancer to tell you all about it.

This method of working with body-awareness is common to many kinds of therapy, but the technique that is most user-friendly is called Focusing, and is described in a book entitled *Focusing* by Eugene Gendlin, published by Bantam, New York, 1981. A more recent book, even more approachable, is *The Power of Focusing: A Practical Guide to Emotional Self-Healing*, by Ann Weiser Cornell, published by New Harbinger Publications, Oakland, CA, 1996. For more information about Focusing, contact: Focusing Resources, 2625 Alcatraz Avenue, #202, Berkeley, CA 94705.

Appendix B

The Astrological Universe

In some ways, this appendix should have been at the beginning of the book, as it deals with the question of what kind of a universe it is in which astrology makes sense. How can it be that we can track and analyze our own patterns of inner energies by observing something as remote as the planets? However, it seemed better to leave this issue until last, so the book can be read and used as a straightforward astrology text. The reader can then accept or reject as much of the metaphysics of this appendix as he or she feels inclined.

As far as a great many people are concerned, of course, astrology does not make sense. They see it as addle-headed superstition, and a great deal of what passes for astrology in the columns of the press offers justification for such a view.

A few months before this writing (1995), one of the leading English "quality" newspapers, *The Times*, ran a piece on astrology based on a comment by an astronomer that astrologers use signs of the zodiac that no longer correspond with the constellations. Every so often, some astronomer makes this "discovery" and comes out with it as though it were a new and telling way of exploding the "superstition" of astrology. So far, so good, but the interesting thing is that the paper subsequently published only letters that were in agreement with the original article. I wrote to them expressing the arguments of this chapter, but the letter was not published. (To be fair, a similar letter I wrote several years ago to one of our tabloid papers, *The Daily Mail*, did get published.)

I'm mentioning this incident because it illustrates the difficulties we have in using astrology. The establishment view is that astrology is rubbish, and the view is so strongly held that people will not listen to any argument to the contrary or even accept that such an argument can exist.

They will not even look at, let alone accept, massive statistical evidence such as that produced by Michel Gauquelin. True, Gauquelin's work doesn't really support astrology as it is practiced, but it does show that the positions of the planets at birth correspond with the kinds of character traits we would expect from astrology. The results of his work have been available for twenty or thirty years and they have not had the slightest impact on the determined ignorance of astronomers and others who call themselves scientists and who shape official opinion.

Those of us who use astrology are in a great difficulty because we have very little community support. We are regarded as self-deluded charlatans by the majority opinion, and this, in itself, creates a lot of stress for anyone practicing astrology. I have elsewhere contrasted the situation of the astrologer with that of the doctor. An individual doctor may or may not be a good one, but he or she does not have to worry about the validity of the profession. An astrologer, on the other hand, is always working within the context of skepticism. However brave a face he or she puts on the matter, the truth is that anyone practicing astrology or using it for themselves is, at some level, on the defensive.

This seriously interferes with the effectiveness of astrology. It could be much more widely and intelligently used than it is. If the rudiments of astrology were taught in schools, for example, everyone would have access to a system of self-knowledge that is certainly very much needed in this stressful and rapidly changing world. A big part of the problem is that astrologers in general have no clear rationale for their discipline. Faced with the skepticism of scientists, we can only say, "Yes, but astrology *works*, if you would only try it."

Of course, they won't try it. They are convinced that statistics and scientific method have shown that there is no validity in astrology. We need to be clear that they are right about this. Astrology is not a science and, at the best, as in the case of the Gauquelin work, statistical studies show only that there is *something* in the idea of the planets being related to psychological characteristics. The ideas that the planets are modified by sign, house, and aspects are, at least as far as I know, not supported by any evidence whatsoever.

To get to the root of the matter, we have to make an effort to understand the idea of "world view." This is not easy because it is like fish trying to understand the concept of "ocean." The fact is that we all live within a kind of ocean of unexamined assumptions about what the world is like, and these assumptions actually create our reality.

To deal with this subject properly would require a book in itself, and I am not here going to try to convince anyone of what I am saying. I am just putting out some ideas that you may find useful as a background to your astrological work and as something to think over for yourself, if you feel inclined.

World views are, from time to time, exploded, and when we look back on an earlier one, we can see how inadequate it was. People now say, "Astrology is rubbish. There is no evidence for it and there is no way that the planets out in space can influence us. And the signs and houses that astrologers use are not even *real!*" A few centuries ago, people said, "Of course the sun goes around the earth. Any fool can see that!" Or, "It's obvious that the earth is flat. If you sail too far you'll fall off the edge, so you'd better not try." Ironically, the people who were saying these things probably believed in astrology!

To put the matter in a nutshell, astrology and science belong to entirely different world views. Astrology belongs to a world view in which, in some way, everything is connected. This kind of world view was the one in place up to about three hundred years ago. Roughly speaking, the unexamined assumptions that people had then were that God had created the world and had allotted everything to its proper place, and that humanity was central to the Divine Plan. The natural world was considered not as something to be exploited, but as there to serve humanity and as symbolic of God.

Within this sort of world view, there was nothing inherently out of place about astrology. Since everything was connected, there was no reason the planets should not correspond with personal characteristics and influence our lives. In fact, astrology was really the psychology of the prescientific world view. There were many people who didn't believe in it, of course, but mainly because they thought it was morally wrong, not physically impossible. There were all degrees of sophistication of understanding of astrology, from crude fatalism to a subtle psychological awareness of the correspondence between the motions of the heavenly bodies and the events of the earthly realm.

As we have seen, some of the important assumptions that went with this world view were shown to be wrong. Copernicus demonstrated that the sun is the center of the solar system and Columbus showed that the earth is a globe. Big changes were under way, and with the Renaissance, the emphasis began to shift to a focus on humanity rather than God.

With Rene Descartes, the French philosopher (1596–1650) the stage was set for the emergence of the modern scientific world view. Descartes' purpose was to develop a totally secure foundation for all knowledge. He set about this by systematically attacking all his beliefs. He came to the conclusion that the only certainty was his own conscious experience, and therefore his own existence. Descartes formulated this basis of his philosophy as "Cogito, ergo sum," "I think, therefore I am." He developed it into the view that consciousness and matter were quite separate. The organic view of the universe was to be discarded and humanity was seen as utterly disconnected from the world of nature.

As Victor Hugo said, "There is nothing more powerful than an idea whose time has come." Descartes' philosophy was such an idea. The Renaissance had stirred up notions about the supremacy of mankind, and the desire to study and conquer nature was very prevalent. Descartes work gave a focus to these ideas and quickly became established as the prevailing world view. This is the modern world view, that all the secrets of nature lie in matter, and that they can be discovered by scientific analysis and used to give us ever-increasing power.

It has been very successful. By the end of the nineteenth century, physics had apparently solved all the major problems, and mankind had at its disposal a degree of power hardly dreamed of. In this world view, astrology makes no sense at all. It *seems*—and I want to stress that word— that astrologers are claiming that the motions of bodies far out in space influence, or at least have some connection with, our states of consciousness and the events of our lives. Since it *seems* abundantly clear from the success of science that Descartes' proposition is the correct one, astrology can be no more than a delusion left over from a previous world view, which has been shown to be wrong.

Notice that this is not something we are ever given the chance to think about or question. We are held within this world view like fish in water. *We take it for granted as the basis of all our thinking!* It is not just an intellectual idea, but a framework or cage in which "we live and move and have our being," to quote the Bible. To shift a world view takes a lot of clarity and determination. Mere evidence that contradicts it does not have any effect. Such evidence is seen as simply a trivial anomaly that has nothing to do with the business of real life. We have seen that Gauquelin has produced massive statistical evidence that astrology at least merits being taken seriously. Even more to the point, science itself has demonstrated beyond all doubt that the Cartesian-split world view is incorrect.

The world of particle physics is a world in which astrology once again makes sense. The one or two minor problems that physics had not solved by the end of the nineteenth century turned out to be disasters for the Cartesian-Newtonian world view. I don't want to get into technical details here. They are, in any case, readily available in a number of popular books on particle physics, especially *The Tao of Physics* by Fritjof Capra and *The Dancing Wu Li Masters* by Gary Zukhav. In essence, what quantum physics has shown is that the apparently solid world of matter does not exist in its own right but is a product of consciousness. Each of us quite literally creates the universe we experience. Everything is connected with everything else, and there is no reason at all why astrology should not work. In fact, given the universe of quantum physics, one would have to deduce that astrology *should* work!

So why doesn't everyone recognize this? Why wouldn't the Letters Editor of *The Times*, who has no doubt read the books on quantum physics, publish my letter pointing out that science itself has now shown that there is a case for taking astrology seriously? Briefly, the answer is in the sheer tenacity of an established world view. If we want to take advantage of the perspective given to us by particle physics, we will have to make the effort to make it a reality in our own lives and consciously disregard the Cartesian universe.

There is a further and more recent extension to the discoveries of quantum physics. This is the idea of the "holographic paradigm" developed by physicist David Bohm and brain scientist Karl Pribram. The theory is that the brain is like a holographic plate. When an actual holographic plate is illuminated by a laser beam, a hologram is produced. So the theory is that the brain is "illuminated" by unknown energies and produces the hologram that is the universe we experience.

This idea gives us the basis of a model of an astrological universe and can be diagrammed as shown on the following page. The region marked E is the primary creative source, about which nothing can be said. This is Infinite Intelligence, God, Supreme Being, Great Spirit, whatever you want to call it. It emanates the "unknown frequencies" that Bohm and Pribram talk about. Among these frequencies are the archetypes of the planets and signs.

Region D is just below conscious awareness. The very abstract ideas the archetypes express are becoming more condensed into form. In fact, they can be seen as the planetary characters doing their jobs. This region can be regarded as being your birth chart, not, of course, in the sense of marks on a piece of paper, but as the idea that the concrete chart represents. In other words, it is the whole potential individual pattern of your life. It may be thought of as the film in a movie projector, except that this film produces a holographic movie complete with smell, taste, and feeling as well as sight and sound.

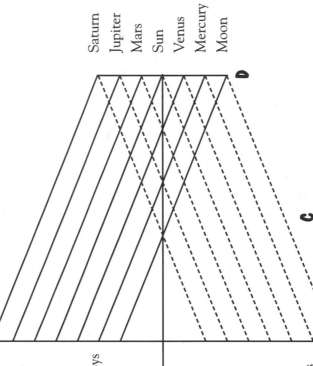

A

Saturn, lead, ice, stones, yew trees
Jupiter, tin, banks, banquets, lawyers
Mars, iron, red, blood, knives
Sun, gold, jewels, kings, film stars
Venus, copper, doves, cakes, lace, girls
Mercury, mercury, messages, agents, boys
Moon, silver, water, inns, tides, women

B

sadness, integrity, weight, hate
jollity, optimism, extravagance
courage, strength, daring, sarcasm
power, ambition, generosity, joy
love, pleasure, ease, courtesy, grace
understanding, skill, ideas, logic, nerves
timidity, intuitions, feelings, kindness

Saturn
Jupiter
Mars
Sun
Venus
Mercury
Moon

E

D

C

The region C is our normal consciousness, and regions A and B contain the objects of which that consciousness is aware. There are two kinds of these objects, sometimes known as "scientific facts" and "poetic facts." Scientific facts are the things we encounter in the external world. Poetic facts are inner feelings and sensations. We often lose sight of the reality that these are just as much objects to consciousness as the external world is because we tend to identify with them more. We see a charging bull as something outside ourselves, but we tend to see the fear it inspires as being "me." Being able to see the fear, or other feelings, as just as much an object of consciousness as the bull is the key to controlling it.

Region A shows the experiences of the external world. It includes a number of examples of what the planetary archetypes "rule" in their concrete form. These include the physical planet, which is shown in bold type. Region B shows the inner effects of the planetary archetypes. So the archetype "Saturn" emanating from the creative source will manifest just below the normal level of consciousness as the energy we call Saturn in astrology and which is represented as being something like an old math teacher in this book. The inner objects, which then emanate from this, are sadness, integrity, weight, and hate, among many others. The outer objects include lead, ice, stones, yew trees, and the planet Saturn itself.

On this model, the physical planets do not influence us. We create them, or they are created through us, by the action of the archetypes on the brain. Astrology works because the planets are like lights on a control board. By observing them we can discover what is going on in us in regions C and D. A conventional astrological analysis enables us to discover what is going on in C. Using the images of the planetary characters enables us to penetrate further and experience what is happening in D. Once we can do that and are no longer stuck in merely thinking about and verbalizing our experience, we can move toward region E, which is the knowledge of God, and totally beyond the scope of this book. Nevertheless, it is the ultimate aim of everyone, and astrology is just one of many means of attaining it.

Readers familiar with the Qabala will realize that the diagram is, in some ways, another form of the Tree of Life figure.

The ideas presented in this appendix are no more than hints, but they can be elaborated into a full, consistent theory of astrology. The planetary characters are a means of making practical use of this theory.

Stay in Touch. . .

Llewellyn publishes hundreds of books on your favorite subjects

On the following pages you will find listed some books now available on related subjects. Your local bookstore stocks most of these and will stock new Llewellyn titles as they become available. We urge your patronage.

Order by Phone

Call toll-free within the U.S. and Canada, **1–800–THE MOON.**
In Minnesota call **(612) 291–1970.**
We accept Visa, MasterCard, and American Express.

Order by Mail

Send the full price of your order (MN residents add 7% sales tax) in U.S. funds to:
> **Llewellyn Worldwide**
> **P.O. Box 64383, Dept. K017–5**
> **St. Paul, MN 55164–0383, U.S.A.**

Postage and Handling

- $4.00 for orders $15.00 and under
- $5.00 for orders over $15.00
- No charge for orders over $100.00

We ship UPS in the continental United States. We cannot ship to P.O. boxes. Orders shipped to Alaska, Hawaii, Canada, Mexico, and Puerto Rico will be sent first-class mail.

International orders: Airmail—add freight equal to price of each book to the total price of order, plus $5.00 for each non-book item (audiotapes, etc.). Surface mail—Add $1.00 per item.

Allow 4–6 weeks delivery on all orders. Postage and handling rates subject to change.

Group Discounts

We offer a 20% quantity discount to group leaders or agents. You must order a minimum of 5 copies of the same book to get our special quantity price.

Free Catalog

Get a free copy of our color catalog, *New Worlds of Mind and Spirit*. Subscribe for just $10.00 in the United States and Canada ($20.00 overseas, first class mail). Many bookstores carry *New Worlds*—ask for it!

Computerized Astrology Reports

Simple Natal APS03-119: Your chart calculated by computer in the Tropical/Placidus House system or the House system of your choice. It has all of the trimmings, including aspects, midpoints, Chiron and a glossary of symbols, plus a free booklet! $5.00

Personality Profile Horoscope APS03-503: Our most popular reading! This ten-part reading gives you a complete look at how the planets affect you. Learn about your general characteristics and life patterns. Look into your imagination and emotional needs. It is an excellent way to get acquainted with astrology and to learn about yourself. **$20.00**

Personal Relationship Reading APS03-506: If you've just called it quits on one relationship and know you need to understand more about yourself before you test the waters again, then this is the report for you! This reading will tell you how you approach relationships in general, what kind of people you look for and what kind of people might rub you the wrong way. Important for anyone! **$20.00**

Compatibility Profile APS03-504: Find out if you really are compatible with your lover, spouse, friend or business partner! This is a great way to get an in-depth look at your relationship with another person. Find out each person's approach to the relationship. Do you have the same goals? How well do you deal with arguments? Do you have the same values? This service includes planetary placements for both individuals, so send birth data for both and specify the type of relationship (i.e., friends, lovers, etc.). Order today! **$30.00**

How to Order Astrological Charts

Use birth certificate for accurate information. Send order by mail. No phone orders, please. Send form with descriptive letter and main concerns. Use additional sheet of paper if necessary. Write or call for information on other reports and services available.

Name of Service   Order #APS03-   Price

_____   _____   _____

_____   _____   _____

BILLING INFORMATION

NAME_____ ADDRESS_____

CITY_____ STATE _____ZIP_____

DAYTIME PHONE (if we have questions)_____

Make checks or money orders payable to Llewellyn Worldwide. Mail to:

    Llewellyn Worldwide
    P.O. Box 64383, Dept. K017–5
    St. Paul, MN 55164–0383, U.S.A.

CHARGE IT! _____ VISA _____ MasterCard _____Am Express

CARD NUMBER_____ EXP. DATE_____

SIGNATURE OF CARDHOLDER_____

ASTROLOGY AND THE GAMES PEOPLE PLAY
A Tool for Self-Understanding in Work & Relationships

Spencer Grendahl

Expand your self-awareness and facilitate personal growth with the Astro-analysis approach to astrology! Astro-analysis is a completely new and unique system that enables you to combine simple astrological information with the three-ring model of basic ego states—Parent, Adult, and Child—used in popular psychology. This easy-to-follow technique makes available to the average person psychological insights that are generally available only to astrologers. Not only is it easy to transcribe your horoscope onto Astro-analysis' three-sphere diagram, but you will find that this symbolic picture provides accurate and meaningful perceptions into the energy patterns of your personality, clearly delineating the areas that may be "overweighted" or most in need of balance. This material is enhanced by examples and explanations of horoscopes of actual people.

Astro-analysis is a powerful self-help tool that will quickly make you aware of the basis for your behavior patterns and attitudes, so you can get a new perspective on your relationships with others and determine the most promising strategies for personal growth.

1-56718-338-7, 224 pp., 7 x 10, softcover $12.95

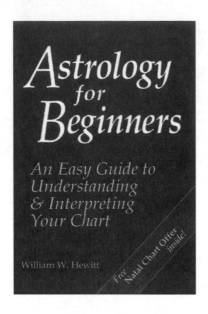

ASTROLOGY FOR BEGINNERS
An Easy Guide to Understanding &
Interpreting Your Chart

William Hewitt

Anyone who is interested in astrology will enjoy *Astrology for Beginners*. This book makes astrology easy and exciting by presenting all of the basics in an orderly sequence while focusing on the natal chart. Llewellyn even includes a coupon for a free computerized natal chart so you can begin interpretations almost immediately without complicated mathematics.

Astrology for Beginners covers all of the basics. Learn exactly what astrology is and how it works. Explore signs, planets, houses and aspects. Learn how to interpret a birth chart. Discover the meaning of transits, predictive astrology and progressions. Determine your horoscope chart in minutes without using math.

Whether you want to practice astrology for a hobby or aspire to become a professional astrologer, *Astrology for Beginners* is the book you need to get started on the right track.

0-87542-307-8, 288 pp., 5¼ x 8, softcover $9.95

THE BOOK OF LOVERS
Men Who Excite Women,
Women Who Excite Men

Carolyn Reynolds

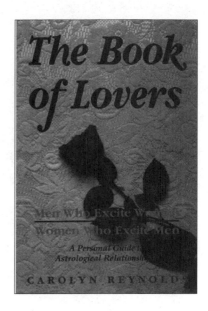

What are you looking for in a lover or potential mate? If it's money, set your sights on a Pisces/Taurus. Is exercise and health food your passion? Then a Virgo/Cancer will share it with you.

Where do you find these people? They're all here, in *The Book of Lovers*. Astrologer Carolyn Reynolds introduces a new and accurate way to determine romantic compatibility through the use of Sun and Moon sign combinations. And best of all, you don't have to know a single thing about astrology to use this book!

Here you will find descriptions of every man and woman born between the years 1900 and 2000. To see whether that certain someone could be "the one," simply locate his or her birthdata in the chart and flip to the relevant pages to read about your person's strengths and weaknesses, sex appeal, personality and most importantly, how they will treat you!

0-87542-289-0, 464 pp., 6 x 9, softcover $14.95

THE INSTANT HOROSCOPE READER
Planets by Sign, House and Aspect

Julia Lupton Skalka

Find out what was written in the planets at your birth! Almost everyone enjoys reading the popular Sun sign horoscopes in newspapers and magazines; however, there is much more to astrology than knowing what your Sun sign is. How do you interpret your natal chart so that you know what it means to have Gemini on your 8th house cusp? What does astrology say about someone whose Sun is conjoined with natal Jupiter?

The Instant Horoscope Reader was written to answer such questions and to give beginners a fresh, thorough overview of the natal chart. Here you will find the meaning of the placement of the Sun, the Moon and each planet in the horoscope, including aspects between the natal planets, the meaning of the houses in the horoscope and house rulerships. Even if you have not had your chart cast, this book includes simple tables that enable you to locate the approximate planetary and house placements and figure the planetary aspects for your birthdate to give you unique perspectives about yourself and others.

1-56718-669-6, 272 pp., 6 x 9, illus.   **$14.95**

WHEN WILL YOU MARRY?
Find Your Soulmate
Through Astrology

Rose Murray

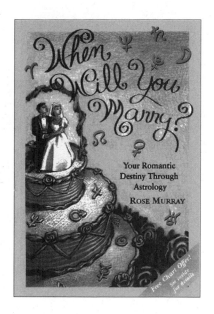

Never before has an astrology book so thoroughly focused on timing as a definitive factor in successful marriage relationships. Written in language the beginner can easily follow, *When Will You Marry?* will engage even the most advanced student of astrology in search of the perfect mate. *When Will You Marry?* guides you through the process of identifying what you need in a marriage partner and the most favorable times to meet that partner based on transits to the natal chart. *When Will You Marry?* then provides clear instruction on comparing your chart with that of a potential mate. This premier match-making method is laid out chapter-by-chapter, with instruction progressing from the basics—like the natal chart and compatible signs—to fine tuning with Sun-Moon midpoints, chart linkups and Arabian parts. By the time the you reach the book's latter parts, you will be able to confirm with great exactness whether or not a particular person is "the one!"

1-56718-479-0, 240 pp., 6 x 9, softbound   **$12.95**

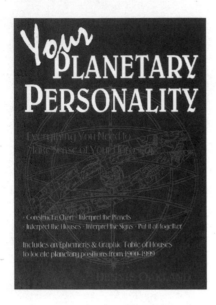

YOUR PLANETARY PERSONALITY
Everything You Need to Make Sense of Your Horoscope

Dennis Oakland

This book deepens the study of astrological interpretation for professional and beginning astrologers alike. Dennis Oakland's interpretations of the planets in the houses and signs are the result of years of study of psychology, sciences, symbolism, Eastern philosophy plus the study of birth charts from a psychotherapy group. Unlike the interpretations in other books, these emphasize the life processes involved and facilitate a greater understanding of the chart. Includes 100-year ephemeris.

Even if you now know nothing about astrology, Dennis Oakland's clear instructions will teach you how to construct a complete and accurate birth chart for anyone born between 1900 to 1999. After you have built your chart, he will lead you through the steps of reading it, giving you indepth interpretations of each of your planets. When done, you will have the satisfaction that comes from increased self-awareness and from being your own astrologer!

This book is also an excellent exploration for psychologists and psychiatrists who use astrology in their practices.

0-87542-594-1, 580 pp., 7 x 10, softcover $24.95